THE HAIRY HIKERS

THE HAIRY HIKERS

Summersdale Publishers Ltd
46 West Street
Chichester
West Sussex
PO19 1RP
UK

www.summersdale.com

Printed and bound in the UK by CPI Group (UK) Ltd, Croydon, CR0 4YY

ISBN: 978-1-84953-237-2

Substantial discounts on bulk quantities of Summersdale books are available to corporations, professional associations and other organisations. For details contact Summersdale Publishers by telephone: +44 (0) 1243 771107, fax: +44 (0) 1243 786300 or email: nicky@summersdale.com.

THE HAIRY HIKERS

A Coast-to-Coast Trek Along the French Pyrenees

DAVID LE VAY

summersdale

ABOUT THE AUTHOR

David Le Vay lives in south-west London. He is a child-therapist and a senior lecturer at Roehampton University, a jazz pianist in a band that gigs regularly around London and a keen cricket player.

For Nicky and Jessica
For being with me every step of the way

And for Rob
Friend and companion

GR10

ENGLAND

Hendaye
St-Jean-Pied-de-Port
St Engrâce
Gourette
Cauterets
Luchon
Corrie Lake
Py
Pic du Canigou

Banyuls Sur Mer

FRANCE

Border

SPAIN

CONTENTS

PROLOGUE

'But I hate walking... I've always hated walking.' My plaintive and frankly rather pathetic cry rang out around the dining room as we sat eating breakfast one fairly ordinary Saturday morning. My partner Nicky looked at me with a combination of concern and irritation whilst Jessica, our daughter, simply raised a curious eyebrow, gave a wry smile and held my arm in the way that you might an elderly gent as you escort him across a busy road.

The cause of my sorry angst was the fact that I was days away from embarking on a two-month, 850-km trek along the entire length of the Pyrenees; coast to coast from the Atlantic to the Mediterranean. I was, for better or worse, about to strike forth along the fabled GR10, a 'Grande Randonnée' footpath that begins in the small town of Hendaye on the Atlantic coast and follows the French side of the Pyrenees eastwards, all the way to Banyuls-sur-Mer on the Mediterranean. Quite why I was doing this I didn't know.

Did I hate walking? Maybe.

Up until this point, the longest walk I had ever undertaken was a 24-km sponsored school walk with my mother across Ashdown Forest in East Sussex when I was twelve. All I remember is that it rained non-stop that day, and after we had finished we sat dripping in the school hall whilst they revived us with hot chicken soup. I had been on some pretty good day-walks since then, maybe four or five hours at the most, but I had never been on any kind of hiking or trekking holiday as such. The nearest I got to this was when, many years ago at the ripe old age of thirty, I decided to go to the Lake District for a week on my own; to walk and 'find myself' in the hills. Unfortunately, I didn't like what I found and lasted only a couple of days (which somehow didn't include a lot of walking) before returning back home with my metaphorical tail between my legs.

I am still not entirely sure where the idea of doing the GR10 originated. No doubt, at the age of forty-three, there was a flavour of mid-life crisis about the whole thing. We didn't have an au pair for me to run away with, I knew I couldn't climb Everest and I wasn't about to circumnavigate the globe on a spacehopper, but the idea of an epic mountain trek seemed both challenging and just about within the realms of possibility. And once this idea had entered my mind it just sat there, percolating for some months like a strong black French double espresso.

I hadn't mentioned anything to Nicky at this stage, although she knew that I was feeling a little stir-crazy and wanted to do something to haul myself, albeit temporarily, out of the clutches of suburbia and my somewhat stressful job as a child-therapist. Over the years I have banged on enough times about buying a house abroad or living on a barge or growing a beard and hiding in the woods down at our allotment, so all in all Nicky was well aware that I had the potential to do something stupid at some point in my life. I stumbled upon the GR10 itself whilst I surfed the Net looking at walking holidays in France, and somehow the idea of a coast-to-coast walk that incorporated mountains, French villages and beautiful scenery seemed just about perfect. I had always had something of a love affair with France, having spent many holidays there both with Nicky and Jess and with friends in my younger days. As for mountains, there is something very special about the intense sensation of height and space, the solitude and sense of escape and the way in which they transform one's perspective, both externally and internally. They have always captivated me.

So, with the idea half forming in my mind, I bought a couple of books on the GR10 and the more I read the more the feeling of wanting to embark on this mad adventure started to creep up on me, to the point where I started to become a little obsessed. I don't know if Nicky saw the book lying around or whether I unconsciously kept it hidden away like some guilty secret, but my actual 'coming out', so to speak, could have been handled a little better. We were on a family holiday in Cornwall for a few days with a good friend of ours, and during a pleasant evening in the local pub over a couple of pints of Frenchman's Creek I suddenly blurted out the fact that I had been thinking about taking two months off work, abandoning the family, buggering off to France and walking miles along some bloody mountains. That's not quite how I put it of course, but it's fair to say that was the gist of the translation kindly provided for me by Nicky. And, to be fair, whilst she didn't oppose the idea, she wasn't too impressed with the cowardly way in which I had told her about it.

Over the next few months the idea continued to crystallise and one evening I mentioned it to my good friend Rob who immediately declared his hand. 'Count me in,' he said. Now, Rob is a lovely chap and a man of many talents: builder, cook, singer and guitarist, alongside a healthy dose of the more quirky and eccentric. Amongst his many talents, he is the world's number one *Chitty Chitty Bang Bang* fan and knows by heart the words to all the songs (to which we have been subjected many times over dinner and a glass or two of red wine). Indeed, one of his numerous alter-egos is Grandpa Potts and his rendition of 'Posh' is very fine. So, when Rob said 'Count me in' I was very glad to have him on board; although I was a little anxious about how the two of us would manage such a long and intimate journey together. However, to be honest, the idea of doing the walk on my own was daunting, both physically and emotionally, so I welcomed the idea of Rob's company. To his credit, he had done a fair bit of long-distance mountain walking and orienteering over the years. Certainly, in this respect, he was much better qualified and equipped for this venture than I was. He also kindly volunteered to be my 'case study' whilst we were away. I wasn't exactly sure what this meant, but I got the strange feeling that he knew something I didn't. Still, I thought, if Oliver Sacks can write *The Man Who Mistook His Wife for a Hat*, I can write *The Man Who Walked the Pyrenees with Grandpa Potts*.

As time passed the idea of the walk slowly became more of a reality in my mind, as opposed to some kind of wishy-washy abstract fantasy. The more people I spoke to about it, the more the possibility became a probability; it was as if the simple act of talking about it was enough to bring it gradually into being. As a therapist I was curious about this process in the context of my work with children, in which I often use stories and narratives to enable a child to begin to make sense of their very troubled experiences. Here I was creating a narrative for myself and ultimately reaching a kind of 'tipping point', wherein I had told enough people to somehow commit myself to having to undertake the journey. The response I got from people when I told them of my plan was varied. Most common was along the lines of: 'Hey brilliant, you'll really lose some weight', which roughly translated as 'You fat git, you'll be lucky to get halfway'. Other people said: 'Make sure you wear a decent hat', for which of course you can read 'You bald idiot, you'll get burnt to death'. Other people seemed envious and some genuinely interested. For many people the idea of the walk seemed to tap into their own fantasies and unfulfilled dreams.

What finally made it real for me was taking the plunge and broaching the idea of taking a couple of months off work with my boss. His first words were: 'You bastard... I've been wanting to do that that for years.' His vicarious pleasure in my venture led him to insist that we record the decision there and then, so that it couldn't be reversed in his absence; it was set down in tablets of stone (well, at least in my supervision notes). This, then, really seemed like it.

In the months that followed, Rob and I went about our slow and rather haphazard business of getting ourselves ready for departure. I was starting from scratch and had to buy boots, rucksack, sleeping bag and all sorts of odd trekking paraphernalia: things like water-purifying tablets, inner socks, a penny whistle and a bright orange survival bag. We would bump into each other in various trekking and camping outlets around town, each wandering around in a GR10-induced daze. I thought I had better get some training in, so I went for a walk in the woods around Ranmore Common in Surrey – and got lost. I also walked up Box Hill, leaving my rucksack in the car because I couldn't be bothered to carry it, and that really was the extent of my preparation. Being self-employed, Rob had to work hard to get together enough money for the trip, so he wasn't able to get much preparation in either. To be honest, the whole affair still felt abstract until I took some decisive action and bought two one-way tickets to Biarritz in the south-west of France. The whole escapade seemed an outrageous, ridiculous idea and as the deadline approached the two of us swung precariously between manic excitement, desperate anxiety and persistent denial.

Walk? What walk?

Then there was the fact that I was going to be away from my family for seven or eight weeks. I had never been away from home for this length of time before and the excitement I did feel was laced with a sense of guilt and unease that perhaps this was all a big mistake. But Nicky and Jessica supported me all the way, gently indulging my grand whim and tolerating all the tedious pre-trek bluster and bouts of self-doubt.

Inevitably, the morning finally came when I awoke to a sudden jolt of anxiety in the pit of my stomach. This was the day. Having made a pact with Rob and a bet with Jess that we wouldn't shave until we reached Banyuls-sur-Mer on the border between France and Spain, I razed my facial stubble to a smooth finish for the last time and then, with a heavy heart and a tear in my eye, waved Jess off to school, knowing I wouldn't see her again for almost two months. Nicky then gave me a lift down to the station where I met Rob, resplendent with his hat and ukulele. Nicky and I hugged as we said our tearful goodbyes, and she gave a last wave and tentative smile as Rob and I waddled and wobbled up the station steps, like two unsightly insects carrying our worldly belongings upon our backs.

ARRIVAL IN HENDAYE

As we sit in the plane on the tarmac at Stansted, waiting for our take-off 'window', the pilot suddenly announces, 'Cabin crew, prepare to land.' The fact that we haven't even left the ground at this point doesn't fill me with confidence. As a somewhat nervous flyer, I like to think that the crew, and especially the pilot, are in full possession of their faculties and at least have a working idea of what they are doing. The fact that our poor pilot does not seem entirely sure whether we are in the air or on the ground immediately pushes my anxiety level up to an early five out of ten.

Take-off is pretty uneventful; although, in my opinion, you can hardly call sitting in a metal tube and being blasted into the air by a pair of massive jet engines uneventful. That's the thing about flying: the whole experience is designed to stop you from thinking about what it is that you are actually doing. Unfortunately, I can't stop myself from thinking about what it is I am actually doing and my general coping strategy is to fixate on the facial expressions of the cabin crew with the aim of detecting any kind of early flight malfunction. Of course, the problem with this strategy is that I begin to resemble a slightly psychotic sweaty terrorist with mad eyes who may be about to blow up the plane at any minute.

As we climb, my anxiety level gradually flattens out (along with the plane) to a manageable three, and with the help of a large gin and tonic falls rapidly to a barely registering one. With a glint in his eye, Rob turns and asks me if I want to 'touch his furry puma' and I shoot up to a rather alarmed nine. I begin to feel a little concerned about the days and weeks ahead; we are only hours into the trip and things have already taken a sinister turn. Thankfully, it turns out he is referring to the little embossed Puma logo on his new shirt. Rob has been struggling with the fact that in the general rush to get organised over the last few days he bought a couple of 'brand' shirts – whatever Rob is, he's not a 'brand' man. Still, he's pleased with his little furry puma, so to speak.

As we fly, we both seem a little lost in our own thoughts. It's hard to believe that after all this time we are actually on our way. I wonder aloud about the idea of getting a taxi tomorrow from Hendaye to Biriatou to save a couple of hours trudging out of town, but Rob is unmoved. He's right, I know, but the idea of a little head start is very appealing. I am also aware that I am already thinking of ways to avoid walking before we have even started.

We file off the plane, pick up our rucksacks and wander outside in search of a taxi to take us to Biarritz station. It's not far, but even Rob agrees that it would have been a dispiriting walk along the hard shoulder of a busy airport road and that we should save ourselves for better times ahead. At the station I have to employ my rusty, schoolboy French for the first time and manage to buy us tickets to Hendaye. Rob's grasp of French is, to be generous, limited and one of the daunting aspects of this trip, apart from climbing a thousand-plus metres every day, is the prospect of having to be the chief communicator. Apart from the language, this is a particular challenge for me, as I am known as something of a 'sociophobe', in the sense that any kind of human interaction tends to instil in me a degree of apprehension. At home I rarely answer the phone and Nicky tears her hair out in frustration when I will do anything to avoid calling on the neighbours to ask them to feed the cat. God knows how I ended up becoming a therapist (or then again, maybe that's exactly how I ended up becoming a therapist). Anyway, I have always relied on Nicky in the past for general 'front of house' activities and I feel uncertain about how I am going to manage over the next couple of months.

We find ourselves with an hour or so to kill at Biarritz station and so, unsurprisingly some may think, decide to fill the time with a couple of beers and a few games of pool. Bang on time, the train for Hendaye pulls in and we run, stumble and haul ourselves aboard, and in a slightly beer-induced cheerful state allow the train to carry us off to our destination. I suspect we both feel a little frisson of anticipation as we pull into Hendaye. This is, after all, the beginning of our great journey. Over the last year or so I have dreamt about, contemplated, even fantasised about this moment.

As we get our bearings, I inform Rob that the only really significant moment in history that this little coastal town can lay claim to is that in 1940 Hitler had a meeting with Franco on this very station platform to discuss Spain's possible involvement in World War Two. Franco remained unconvinced apparently, but it is strange to think of the places that played some part in the shaping of history. Rob is mildly interested but does not seem too impressed with my little factoid, probably because he knows I have just read it in our guidebook.

After taking a couple of pictures outside the station, we haul on our packs and head off to find somewhere to stay. In keeping with my fairly laissez-faire attitude to life I had told Rob that we didn't need to book ahead, as we were out of season and it would be easy to find a room in a cheapish hotel down on the seafront with the help of Douggie, our guide. Douglas Streatfeild-James is the author of *Trekking in the Pyrenees*, our guidebook of choice, and will be our friend, foe and virtual third companion over the next two months. Famous last words, of course. Our first-choice hotel is surrounded by scaffolding and loitering French workmen puffing on cigarettes. *'Fermé!'* they shout, with unconcealed amusement, in response to our inquiring looks. The next couple of places we try are also either closed or full, and so it's with some relief when we stumble into a place with a very kindly female proprietor who says she has one room left.

She leads us up a couple of flights of stairs to a bedroom at the end of a long corridor, opening a door with a flourish to reveal a small room with a solitary bed in the middle. Rob and I exchange anxious looks, each expressing the same unsaid question: are we ready for such intimacy at this early stage in our adventure? In the face of our uncertainty we say a polite *'non merci'* and head back down to reception. Still, our exceptionally kind hostess seems determined to help us and after a flurry of frantic phone calls informs us that there is a two-bedroom, self-contained apartment just across the road, and if we are happy to wait for an hour or so they will get it cleaned and ready. That sounds good to us, so at the invitation of our hostess we throw down our packs, get a drink and sink into the comfy armchairs in the hotel bar.

The other seats are occupied by some friendly elderly folks, two women and a man, who seem genuinely perplexed and somewhat amused by our presence. We attempt to engage in a conversation of sorts, aided by much frantic gesturing and arm waving. The Monsieur in particular is holding court and seems to be laughing uproariously at his own jokes, which of course we don't understand. Our hostess and a younger woman who, it transpires, is her daughter turn up and join in the laughter, which at this point we gather is being mostly directed at us. Our hostess beckons us over: 'He's a comedian,' she whispers. Monsieur le Comédien then goes through an elaborate series of gestures, which ends with the very explicit suggestion that we should go upstairs and have sex with the hostess' daughter. Everyone laughs, so that's all right then, but we gracefully decline the kind invitation and manage to get the conversation around to the slightly safer topic of rugby. After a short while of pretending we know what we are talking about we get the all-clear from Madame and with some relief make a hasty retreat across the road and up to our very own little apartment.

After a pointless bit of settling-in behaviour – turning the television on and off, opening and closing all the cupboards and some totally unnecessary flatulence (is this some kind of male territorial rite?) – we decide to head out to downtown Hendaye to find something to eat. We agree we must have *moules frites*, and after a little mooching around we find a good-looking place right by the seafront. It's perfect and we each get stuck in to a huge cauldron of mussels in cream, accompanied by chips, bread and a couple of carafes of red wine. Strangely, there is some extremely frenetic piano playing in the background, which makes us feel like we are taking part in a kind of Gallic culinary challenge on an ancient episode of Bruce Forsyth's *Generation Game*.

A couple of glasses of wine later, the piano-playing begins to slow down and I get the urge to smoke, so I go out on a mad dash to hunt down some Camel cigarettes. Rob has decided to temporarily give up smoking, but only being an occasional smoker myself I have a small vested interest in him keeping up his habit, which isn't particularly the kind of positive reinforcement that he really needs. I wonder if this slightly dysfunctional pattern of mutual smoking dependency is something that will accompany us throughout the trip.

Exhausted and a little merry we get back to the apartment and collapse into bed. I speak briefly with Nicky and Jess on the phone and they simultaneously sound just round the corner and a million miles away. As I finish writing the first entry into my new moleskin notebook I get a text from my friend Rupert. It feels good to hear these friendly voices from home: the thought of embarking on this walk tomorrow seems totally unreal and I wonder what I am doing here. Rob is asleep already and the sound of snoring starts to resound around the little apartment. Hmm, it's going to be a long two months.

DAY 1

HENDAYE TO BIRIATOU

Waking to the momentarily disorienting feeling of 'Where the hell am I?', I become aware of a strange kind of deep growling sound and wonder for a moment if somehow a small dog has got into the room. But no, it's Rob of course, still snoring like a trooper. I feel pretty exhausted having slept fitfully, so get up and do a pointless bit of rummaging in my rucksack, not knowing quite what I am looking for. Maybe it was the mussels last night, but my stomach feels a little fragile and so I head to the toilet for a rather noisy and unpleasant ten minutes. At least Rob is still asleep, I think, conscious of my bowel movements, but then I hear him groaning and shouting something about keeping the noise down and that he hasn't heard anything quite so terrible for a long time.

So this is it: the first day of two months of solid walking. It's pissing down outside and I feel daunted and a little nervous. My greatest worry at the moment is the state of my back, which has been giving me quite a bit of trouble over the last few weeks. A fear has been lurking at the back of my mind that I might have to finish the walk early due to back problems, though Rob and I have discussed the possibility of finding masseurs and chiropractors along the way. Rob seems a little too interested in the possibility of a friendly massage (*'Le fin agréable, monsieur?'*). Still, it's no good worrying about that now. Following Rob's lead, I dig out the small pot of Vaseline from my rucksack and prepare myself for what proves to be one of the most soothing and pleasurable physical rituals of the weeks to come. No, it's not what you think. I'm talking about the daily practice of rubbing Vaseline into my toes and feet to prevent the possibility of blisters – one of the best bits of advice I have ever been given. There is indeed something quite gratifying and soothing about the process and added to this is the somewhat contemplative element to the task, which helps prepare the mind and body for the travails ahead.

Feet done and boots on we engage in a final bit of mutual sack rummaging (that's not what you think either) and head across the road for breakfast. Our kind hostess ushers us in and, lo and behold, we find that our compère for the morning is our friend Monsieur le Comédien. Once again he seems much amused by our presence and goes into a long routine that ends with something about us 'pissing *dans les pantalons*'. It's with some relief that we finish our breakfast and say our farewells. Rob admits that he was quite attracted to our hostess, in a motherly kind of way. Remembering his offer to be my 'case study', I make a mental note about Freud and Oedipal complexes.

Hendaye, seen in the half-light of this rather wet morning, seems a fairly non-descript and somewhat unprepossessing kind of place. The town is split into two parts, the main town, Hendaye-Ville, where we walked down from the station yesterday, and Hendaye-Plage, the more touristy area that stretches along the sandy strip of beach. Being the most south-westerly town in France and a good launch pad for both France and Spain, with a nice coastline and child-friendly beaches, it probably is a popular resort in the holidays; but standing here outside the hotel with the cold rain drumming on our ponchos like Ginger Baker we aren't quite seeing Hendaye in all its Atlantic glory. Looking out to sea the Jumeaux rocks are visible: two distinguished columns of rock rising proudly from the water, long eroded and carved off from their parent cliff. A few small fishing boats make their slow passage across the bay, perhaps on their weary way back to the fishing port of Caneta after a long night on the nets.

The fact that Hendaye pretty much sits on the border at this south-western Pyrenean gateway means that it has had its fair share of trouble over the last few hundred years – being reduced to rubble on several occasions after being caught up in cross-border conflicts. The Treaty of the Pyrenees was signed in Hendaye in 1659 to end the Franco–Spanish War. Another interesting snippet of information about this town is that it is home to the 'Hendaye Cross', a 3 m-high carved stone cross that can be seen in the town square. It is apparently something of a holy grail for doom-merchants, in that the carved symbols on the cross are supposedly some kind of cryptic code, which if deciphered spell out a catastrophic end to the world. Well, let's just hope that nobody deciphers it in the next couple of months, otherwise Rob and I are buggered. Where's Tom Hanks when you need him?

After a bit of stocking up at the local supermarket, in which we weigh ourselves down with several pounds of chocolate and dates (just in case we become trapped on a cliff edge for several weeks in a blizzard that has blown away all the bread, cheese and sausage we have also crammed into our laden rucksacks), we set out in the rain to try and find the official start of the GR10; which Douggie tells us is by the casino building at the seafront. We amble around for a good half an hour, looking like bedraggled hunchbacks in our all-weather ponchos, before we discover that the casino is in fact the place where we had our meal last night. Seen in the light of day it's an impressive building, late-nineteenth-century and somewhat Moorish in design, though no longer home to any gambling. Having finally discovered our official start point we walk down onto the beach for a quick photo opportunity: a picture of our bare, wrinkled feet in the sea. The water isn't too cold but the sea itself is a murky grey, reflecting the dismal sky overhead. Hopefully, the next time we are standing like this in the sea it will be the warmer, bluer waters of the Mediterranean. And so it is with a twinge of apprehension that we put back on our socks and boots, take a final gasp of briny sea air, face south-eastwards and take the first faltering steps of our great 850-km journey.

This first day should involve a 'relatively straightforward' six-hour stint to Olhette, where we plan to stay in a *gîte d'étape*. These are the basic hostels and bunkhouses that tend to lie somewhat off the beaten track and are frequented by hikers, cyclists and other assorted travellers. However, with all our dithering it's nearly midday and Rob suggests that we just walk the couple of hours to Biriatou and then get ready for a good early start tomorrow. The plan sounds good to me, so we slowly make our way out of Hendaye. Slowly really is the operative word here, as we get hopelessly lost and can't seem to find our way out of this bloody town. We spend a good two hours walking in circles trying to find the red and white GR10 markers that indicate the trail and I'm starting to feel wet and a little miserable and begin to wish that we had got that taxi to Biriatou. On two occasions a car pulls up and we are offered a lift to where the 'real mountains' begin, but Rob insists that we walk. He's right; we would only be cheating ourselves and feel the worse for it down the line, so – with a few groans – I plod on.

Eventually, we make our way out of town, crossing over the N10 and under the motorway. As the countryside opens up around us it is a relief to leave behind the wet concrete and the sound of cars speeding their way across the border into Spain. We both immediately start to feel better – in fact, not just better, good. This is it; we're walking into the foothills of the Pyrenees, being enveloped by the mountains with a stunning view of the Atlantic coastline to our left. It still feels totally surreal to think we have even got to this point and I am relieved that the trek has finally begun. As we walk we amuse ourselves with a first French lesson for Rob, although considering the poor quality of my own French I use the word 'lesson' very loosely. My initial tactics amount to just hitting him with a few interesting words to juggle with and it works quite well. We cover *'bouilloire'* (kettle) *'sanglier'* (wild boar) and *'souris'* (mouse), which for starters isn't too bad, and Rob is quickly away with the task of putting them into a useful sentence – *'Le sanglier est dans la bouilloire.'*

To be fair, whilst it is good to get out of the town, this first stage of the walk is not that exciting and we can understand why several of the books that we have read say that it is not until you pass Biriatou that the real walking begins. Still, the morning rain has eased off and a cattle track leads us away from the coast and through woods and fields, the cows following our progress with disinterest. The rain has left freshness in the air that adds to the enjoyment of the lush green hills spread out before us. The path is easy going and we climb barely more than 150 m as we make our way up towards the village.

We've been walking for a couple of hours and Rob's kettle is getting rather full with wild boar, so it's with some relief that we stroll into Biriatou and book into the only, and considerably expensive, hotel. Biriatou is a pleasant, quiet village nestling on the edge of a low-lying hill that rises gradually eastward to form the very modest 'mountain' of Xoldokogaina, which sits at a gentle 486 m. It's certainly an evocative name, sounding more like it belongs in Greece or perhaps an episode of *Xena: Warrior*

Princess. The village is dominated by a large church that rises up majestically from a surrounding cluster of white buildings with their distinctive terracotta roof tiles and brown shutters, and from the height of the impressive church steps you get a sweeping view of the Bidasoa Valley.

We spend a relaxing few hours sitting around watching the locals play *pelote* in the *fronton*, the large outside court that dominates this and all other villages in the Basque region. *Pelote* (or *pilota* in its Basque form) is a little like a large-scale, outside version of squash and is clearly taken very seriously by the locals. We watch some youngsters play for a while, who use a small wooden bat known as a *pala* or *paleta* to strike the ball against the large stone wall of the court. Later, a very serious and rather burly guy comes along alone to practise and he dispenses altogether with the need for a bat and just uses his cupped hand. I sense that Rob wants to get down there and give him a game but, perhaps rather wisely, decides to postpone his *pilota* playing debut until another time. But it's very pleasant, sitting here on the wall above the *fronton* court, listening to the sound of the children's laughter and the regular, keen thwack of the leather ball against the stone wall. The sun even puts in a late afternoon appearance and there is a real sense of entering a different world, a different culture. Certainly the Basque Country, which straddles the French–Spanish border at this western end of the Pyrenees, has a strong sense of difference about it. The distinct blend of French and Spanish – the language, fierce traditions, regional food and of course the warm and wet sea climate – creates a rich, vibrant culture that we look forward to engaging with further as our trek proceeds.

We go for a wander around the outskirts of the village and I get the fright of my life when a dog leaps out at me, causing me to jump at least a couple of feet in the air and perform what Rob later christens 'Dave's Dog Dance of Biriatou'. He is of course highly amused by my pathetic behaviour, more so because the dog is chained up behind a fence at the time. Dogs aren't my strong point, I tell Rob, and appoint him as my official canine guardian for the rest of the walk. The idea of a 'dog dance' is something that could probably catch on in these parts. Apparently, there is an old traditional festival in Biriatou called the 'Goose Day' *(Antzar Jokoa)* that takes place each November. The ritual involves villagers on horseback galloping along the main street and pulling the neck of a (dead) goose that has been hung high up on a wire stretched across the street. Sounds fun.

DAY 2

BIRIATOU TO OLHETTE

Af
fter a good breakfast of toast, croissants, ham and cheese, washed down with a couple of cups of strong coffee, we set out on what should be a pretty solid seven-hour stretch. We will be covering about 20 km today and, although the height we have to climb is only around 500 m, it will be a good tester for what's to come. I slept badly last night due to a combination of Rob's snoring (which is, strangely enough, beginning to sound like an angry *sanglier* in a kettle) and my own partial insomnia. As we walk, we are both struck by the lushness of the Basque countryside that gives off a verdant glow. The experience still feels new enough that I don't feel bothered by the weight of my rucksack or the physical effort of walking. As we leave Biriatou the lane sweeps down the village below the church and then turns into a rougher footpath that begins to climb quite steeply up towards the Col d'Osin.

We pass through wooded valleys and alongside a lively stream that tumbles down from the hills above. There is a reassuring comfort about the sound of the water as it gurgles and chatters its way past us and the beginnings of some early morning sunlight flits through the leaves of the overhanging trees, picking out points of light on the water. As we walk, I am reminded of the hours I spent as a child playing in the river that ran close to our house, catching bullheads and stone-loaches in jam jars and taking them home as trophies to impress my elder brothers. We pick our way along the wet, stony path, occasionally jumping large stepping-stones that are carpeted in velveteen, pale green lichen, and tendrils of moss hang beard-like from the trees by the stream's edge. Where the path leads us up and out of the valley to a more open vista we catch glimpses of the Atlantic, a reminder of how close we still are to the coast. We are getting the hang of the distinctive red and white GR10 markers now and Rob is acquainting himself with the maps and acquiring a good sense of the route ahead. The route markers consist of a white stripe above a red stripe daubed on a tree, fencepost, rock, sheep or anything else that seems to have been available at the time. Where there is some doubt about the route, for example at a fork in the path, a red and white cross signals that you have gone the wrong way. Of course, the GR10 is just one of the several hundred Grande Randonnée trails; a network of long-distance paths that criss-cross much of Europe. In France alone the trails cover approximately 60,000 km; that's a lot of walking.

We make our way over the Col d'Osin where a friendly sign points out that it is only another three hours and twenty minutes to Olhette. Still, it feels manageable. The path drops down briefly and then there is quite a stiff climb up to the summit of Mandalé, which peaks at 573 m. The views from here are great, with the Atlantic still forming an aquamarine backdrop behind us and the green hills opening up ahead. The sun continues to burn off the dampness from yesterday's rain and it is with a spring in our step that we begin to drop down from the hills towards Venta d'Inzola, a settlement that straddles the border between France and Spain.

It's an odd little place, which in times gone by was probably quite a lively cross-border market that no doubt relished its duty-free tax status. As it is, it seems rather tacky, with a number of shops lining the single road selling cheap tat, food, booze and cigarettes. I do, however, find myself a good-looking walking stick, which immediately gives me a sense of comfort and security. Donald Winnicott, the renowned psychotherapist, would perhaps have called it a 'transitional object' – and in a way it does provide me with a sense of emotional security and help me manage this temporary separation from my family. It also makes me feel like my father, who always walked with a stick in his latter years.

After buying some bread and *brebis* cheese we sit eating lunch and drinking coffee and both feel pretty good, especially as this is our first experience of stepping across the border into Spain, albeit by a few feet. It does, however, make us pleasingly aware of the way the GR10 pretty much follows the French–Spanish border and we hope for more of these little cross-border forays. The local *brebis* is particularly good. Made from ewe's milk, it has a thick, yellowy-orange rind whilst the ivory body of the cheese itself is firm, smooth and compact. It has a rich, strong and slightly nutty flavour and lends itself very well to being eaten in large chunks with our rustic bread and energising coffee, although I suspect it would also go down very well with a glass of fine red wine. This Basque speciality is apparently particularly good in the late spring and early summer when it has a fragrant, floral quality due to the abundance of flowers that grow in the meadows of the grazing sheep.

The sun is out and Rob suddenly realises that he left his hat back in the hotel room at Biriatou. He's pretty gutted at his loss;

particularly because he has (so he says) an unusually large and oddly shaped head, meaning it is very hard to get a hat that fits. Still, he tries to leave his disappointment behind him, a bit like his lost hat in fact, and makes it his mission to find a new one along the way. I try to impress him with my stick but he's not too interested. Rob, perhaps trying to compensate for the loss of his headwear, tries to persuade me that we should sleep in the Basha tomorrow night. 'Basha' is a Malay word meaning 'shelter' or 'hut' and is essentially an army issue bit of canvas and groundsheet that was given to Rob by a friend.

Apparently it can serve as an emergency tent when need be, using cord to attach it to a nearby tree, or in our case a couple of walking sticks. I am not exactly taken with the idea of sleeping in the open under some green bit of cloth and not sure that our present circumstances count as an emergency, but I can sense this is going to become something of a running theme as Rob likes a spot of wild camping whilst I tend to prefer a nice warm domesticated hotel, given half a chance.

Anyway, suitably fed and watered we stride on, making our way along the road and away from the shops and relative civilisation of Venta d'Inzola. The tarmac road soon gives way to a rough stone-strewn footpath and after crossing a stream we make the last short climb of the day up to the Col du Grand Descarga. Is it so called because it looks a bit like a big snail, I wonder? From here the path traverses the side of the valley, taking us though woodland, bracken and gorse, and the gentle downward trajectory makes for easy walking at a decent pace. The red-brown earth of the path, sprinkled with grey stone, contrasts with the abundant green of the countryside as it snakes its way downward and the air is fresh and invigorating. Every now and again we pause just to take in the view, breathe in the air and relish the simple beauty of the open landscape as it stretches out around us. It doesn't feel like long before we drop down into more woodland and make our way towards the little village of Olhette.

As we approach the village we see what must be the gîte on our left, and lo and behold the woman proprietor beckons us over with a shrill shout, clearly not wanting to miss out on passing trade. This being our first experience of a *gîte d'étape* we are not too sure what to expect, but it's fine: pretty basic but with a good kitchen to cook in and enough bunk beds to sleep about fourteen people. Among the good handful of fellow trekkers, ten or twelve perhaps, there is a bit of mutual sizing-up going on and surreptitious checking out of rucksacks and footwear. We keep pretty much to ourselves and Rob cooks up a good dinner of pasta and sausage whilst everyone else disappears to the main farmhouse for the '*demi-pension*' meal provided by the family running the gîte. After eating we sit outside in the garden to enjoy the lovely evening watching kites soaring high in the sky and listening to a virtual orchestra of little birds singing in the bushes nearby. It's a peaceful, tranquil spot with just the low murmur of our fellow trekkers to disturb the peace. As the light fades around 9.30 p.m. we decide to call it a day and clamber into our bunks, where I acquaint myself for the first time with my sleeping bag and assorted night-time paraphernalia. It feels strange to be sharing a room with strangers; I pull the hood of the sleeping bag over my head and prepare for the long night ahead.

DAY 3

OLHETTE TO AÏNHOA

I wake up feeling rough and tired. Rob's still asleep so I get up and mooch around self-consciously, pretending that I know what I am doing when really I am just trying to cope with the newness of the situation. A few people are up and about, whispering, rustling, brushing teeth, going to the toilet. I manage to get some coffee together by surreptitiously stealing some from a jar in the kitchen when no one is looking. I go back to bed for a bit and doze for a while and then get up again a little later. Rob is up and about and we are suddenly aware that everyone has disappeared again. Having paid the extra few euros for *petit déjeuner* we loiter around waiting for some breakfast-like event to kick in but there's little sign of activity. Eventually, we put two and two together and realise that everyone has buggered off to the farmhouse for their *petit déjeuner*. How is it that everyone else always seems to know more than we do? I have a vague sense it might have something to do with the fact that we got up at least two hours later than everyone else. We stumble into the dining room where a few people are left finishing off their breakfast. Some bits of dried bread remain scattered around the table amongst a few pot of homemade jam. The coffee is warm and the milk all gone. I feel like I haven't yet learned the rules of how all this stuff works and simple tasks like going to find our Madame to ask for replenishments all seem a bit daunting. We exchange a few pleasantries with our remaining fellow trekkers, but mostly keep our heads down and try not to break our teeth on the toast.

Back in the gîte we go through our ritual bit of sack-rummaging. Rob says something about needing to go to the toilet and then asks me if he can use some of my Vaseline. I catch a curious glance from a chap across the room, which suggests he is wondering whether he has stumbled across a Pyrenean version of *Brokeback Mountain*. To make matters worse, Rob then disappears for his morning ablutions, only to awkwardly reappear a minute or so later to announce that the toilet paper has run out and can I go and get some from Madame in the farmhouse. I trudge over to the farmhouse, which now seems deserted, and have to shout feebly up the stairs a few times to where I can hear a little bit of childlike activity. Moments later Madame comes striding down the stairs.

'Er… *bonjour, Madame.*'

'*Oui?*' she says, formidably. The possibility, on this third day, of putting together an adequate sentence in French to cover the matter in hand (or not in hand, in Rob's case) seems remote.

'Er… *le papier… pour la toilette.*' Unbelievably, and to my shame, I find myself doing a brief (but probably much too long) bottom-wiping mime to the large Madame who stands before me. For a moment, I think she might grab my hand and whisk me upstairs to change my pants along with the other children I can hear whimpering up on the first floor somewhere.

'*Ah, un moment,*' she says, disappearing upstairs and then returning with half a roll of toilet paper, no doubt snatched from the very bottoms of babes. Slightly shame-faced, I offer a quiet '*Merci*' and, thankfully, make my escape back to the gîte where I hand over the booty to a grateful Rob who is loitering, buttocks clenched, outside the toilet. Eventually, at least an hour after everyone else has left, we get it together to set off, crossing the little stream at the end of the track and beginning the day's climb.

The first stage of today's walk will take us up and over the 900-m La Rhune and then drop down to the small town of Sare, approximately three hours away in Douggie Time. Douggie Time, it seems, is at least two hours ahead of Greenwich Mean Time – that Douggie's a fit bastard. I don't know if our esteemed guide ran the entire length of the GR10 but his timings for each section do seem very impressive and somehow I think we are going to be lagging behind his pace. The first bit feels pretty good and, although it's a long, hot slog, once we drop over the Col des Trois Fontaines, just below the summit of La Rhune, we know that the day's climbing is done. I start to get a real feel of being up in the mountains and at the peak we come across fields of horses with bells around their necks, frolicking in the grass. We also see some more black kites wheeling around majestically, high in the sky above us. We then unexpectedly cross the path of a dainty little wooden train trundling its way down from the summit – a pleasant distraction from the exertions of the morning's walking. This, apparently, is the Petit Train de la Rhune: a metre-gauge rack railway that runs the 5 km or so from the Col de Saint-Ignace to the top, but with a top speed of just over 8 km per hour it's not much of a match for us. We wave to the few people aboard, who look like they are enjoying their gentle excursion.

The mountain of La Rhune itself holds something of a mythical status within Basque folklore and whilst we didn't make it to the very peak ourselves (the GR10 rarely goes over any actual peaks – it takes you over the col or the saddle between the peaks – and let's face it, any off-piste adventure that involves more climbing is unlikely), it's apparently home to an impressive array of Neolithic monuments. Perhaps as a consequence, La Rhune developed a reputation as a meeting place for witches who used to gather together to drink strange potions, cast spells and generally get up to a bit of supernatural mischief. The story goes that the local villagers, living in fear of said witches, paid for a monk to live permanently on top of the mountain to keep them away. I like the idea of the monk. Being a hermit has always been my number-one dream job. OK, long hours perhaps, but the perks are good: your own cave, nice view, extended lunch breaks…

As we make our descent we see 4.5 m-high boulders lying along the wayside, as if they had been cast aside by some irate mountain giant. Rob is interested in the geology of the landscape and these rocks are clearly evidence of glacial erosion. As we stride down the hill Rob trips over but expertly cushions his fall by rolling dramatically and ending up lying backwards on top of his rucksack like some kind of flipped-over beetle. He does this a lot apparently, so I look forward to the next one. As we walk, I tell Rob that he was talking a lot in his sleep, although the only thing I heard clearly was something about death and dying. He then tells me he had a dream about being stabbed. I get a sense that his offer to be my case study for the walk was not entirely tongue-in-cheek, but my therapist mind has been left far behind and I am stuck for any meaningful contributions apart from 'Hmm, yeah, that sounds a bit weird'. I knew all the years of training were worth it.

The track drops down through woods and fields, past farms and across gentle streams and it's not long before we arrive in Sare. It's a peaceful little village with pretty whitewashed buildings and distinctive red and green shutters, and we both look forward to a chance to put our feet up and have a bit of a breather as the day is starting to warm up considerably. We exchange a few words with a young couple that we saw in the gîte last night. They are nice Scottish folks who have got lost and can't find their way out of town, so Rob, with the help of the map, sends them on their way whilst we stop for lunch and a rest. As we sit on a wall eating our bread and pâté I start to take my boots off to give my feet a bit of air. Rob tells me that if I take my boots off my feet will swell up and I will never get them on again – ever. I decide to leave them on.

As we've been walking we have been struck by the distinct style of the Basque houses. They are clearly a very house-proud people; all the properties look immaculately maintained and in pristine condition. It seems that the Basque farmhouse, or *etxea*, holds an important place in Basque culture. Apparently, when a house has been finished and the final roof tile put in place, a sprig of bay leaves is traditionally tucked away within the eaves above the front door and the house is given its family name. The houses stay with the family for generations, being passed down to the children and rarely sold. In fact, the Basque home appears to represent a place of sanctuary for the family, a source of honour and pride, and it seems that in times gone by it really was beyond the reach of the law, so that any family members who had fallen foul of the local *gendarmes* were able to hole up for as long as they could manage. It's nice though, the idea of the family home as something sacred, to be held onto and passed down for perhaps many generations. All too often houses are just a piece of real estate, bricks and mortar with a price tag. Maybe when I get back to my own home I will climb up on the roof and stick a sprig of bay leaves under the tiles above the porch. At least I will have somewhere to claim sanctuary next time I get done for speeding on the A3.

The rest of the day is an absolute killer of a road walk; dead flat and in the blinding heat of the mid-afternoon sun. Douggie has the stretch from Olhette to Aïnhoa down for about six hours, but overall we walk about ten hours today and I can't recall ever having walked so far in my life, except perhaps the infamous sponsored walk I did with my mother when I was twelve. My rucksack becomes a monster, pulling and digging into me and causing pain in places I have never felt before. Occasionally, after I fumble to adjust the straps, it sits well on my back and seems to fit like a glove, but mostly I hate it. Of course, it actually fits nothing like a glove, because it's on my back and the idea of wearing rucksacks on my hands is just plain ridiculous. Excuse my attack of pedantry. Still, I love my stick and feel myself becoming deeply attached to it.

Rob pushes on at pace, determined to keep to our schedule, which at the moment consists of taking longish breaks to avoid having to take a rest day until we have got the first week under our belt. I gently chide him for his sergeant major-like tendencies and suggest that we slow down and relax a little but he is a driven man, although by what I am not quite sure. Saying that, though, I wouldn't pass up the chance to be a driven man right now: a farmer's battered old Renault 4 would do nicely. At one point we do pass an old guy with a golden tooth who laughs heartily when we tell him we are walking all the way to the Mediterranean, as if it is the funniest thing he has heard all week (and it probably is for that matter). After a gruelling final uphill climb we eventually arrive in Aïnhoa and stagger into the first open bar we see for a cold beer. I feel totally shattered and ache all over. After downing our drinks we walk into the village to find our next gîte.

Aïnhoa is a sterile place – all very pretty but also lifeless and without character, and the only shops seem to be touristy artisan places that are not a lot of use for your average trekker, or your average local for that matter. Apparently, it is known as one of the most beautiful villages in France, but we are too knackered to appreciate its aesthetic qualities. We are not your average tourists and would much prefer a decent bit of local character. We walk at least another mile or so only to find that the *gîte d'étape* doesn't exist anymore, seemingly having been turned into a private house. I feel on the verge of collapse but Rob suggests we find a campsite and try sleeping in the Basha. For the second time we experience a clash of trekking ideology, as I would rather stump up the thirty quid for a hotel room and a chance for a decent shower and comfortable bed. My initial plan had been to travel as light as possible, avoid any kind of camping at all and stay in gîtes and the odd cheap hotel along the way. Rob, to his credit, is a camper through and through and would prefer a night under the stars in a field to a hotel any day. Still, in my present state of exhaustion I push for the hotel and Rob gracefully relents. I feel like some kind of pathetic, soft, middle-class whinger – and, in fact, that's exactly what I am. But then I wonder if it is really so decadent to want a night in a decent bed after an exhausting ten-hour, 21-km mountain walk. We stagger back into town and book into a hotel and I feel slightly vindicated by the fact that our fellow walkers for the day have all done the same thing. We chat briefly to the Scottish couple and say hello to an elegant-looking French woman who has also been walking the GR10.

After a glorious and much-needed bath in our hotel room (the shower didn't work), and also much-needed washing of pants and socks, we head out for a couple of beers. In the bar we have a 'clearing the air' chat to deal with the little bit of tension that has developed over the last couple of hours. Rob seems worried that I might be starting to think about throwing in the towel after the effort of the day's walk, and to be honest I do wonder how long I will manage to carry on if it continues to feel this difficult. However, the recuperative powers of a bath and a beer or two are quite remarkable and I feel pretty good. It has to be said that when you hit your rhythm the walking does feel great. There is a contemplative quality to the metronomic timing of the feet and, even at this relatively low-level stage, the scenery is stunningly beautiful. We eat in the hotel restaurant, which is too posh and expensive for both our liking but is the one and only eatery in the village, and then collapse in our beds.

DAY 4

AÏNHOA TO BIDARRAY

I wake up feeling shit, having slept badly in the hotel bed, and wonder if I might have had a better night in the Basha, although I daren't mention this to Rob. After getting ourselves packed and ready we have another fairly nondescript breakfast of coffee, toast and jam with the odd croissant thrown in and head out for the day. We also catch sight of the French woman who walked the same stage as us yesterday. She has just been handed a pile of clothes, all obviously freshly laundered and pressed. Blimey, she's really doing the GR10 in style.

As we start walking I feel a little better; there's something about being on the move that always makes me feel more at ease and less troubled. Going by Douggie Time, it's a six-and-a-half-hour stretch today with an overall climb of around 700 m, but we have learned by now that we can add at least a couple of hours on to Douggie's estimates. The initial climb is a seriously steep 500 m and we slowly plod up to the first high-point, which is the Col des Trois Croix. As the name suggests, there are three enormous crosses planted in the ground by a small stone chapel called the Chapelle de l'Aubépine. The crosses come with obligatory crucified figures attached. From here, we can look down and see Aïnhoa below us and we are surprised at how quickly we have gained height in just this first half-hour or so.

A little further on we disturb a group of six or seven vultures that launch themselves dramatically into the air close above our heads. They are amazing birds; huge and slightly prehistoric as they haul themselves into the sky with slow flaps of their great wings and then circle effortlessly in the warm thermals that push up from below. The trail is great today, easy walking with incredible open vistas that for the first time give us a real sense of remoteness as we move away from the more populous coastal region. From here, there are a series of three fairly gentle climbs, rather than the more brutal 'one up, one down' sections that seem to be a feature of the days ahead, and the effect is of being on a plateau with long sections of slight descent that are perfect for walking. The weight of my rucksack combined with the motion of my movement and gentle descent of the path just seems to propel me along effortlessly.

We walk for hours and don't see another soul, that is until we come to a little *gîte d'étape* in the middle of nowhere, just to the west of the Col des Veaux. Here we stumble across our Scottish friends again who are tucking into a tasty looking three-course meal. They are clearly working on a slightly different plan to us. We had considered stopping here for the night but as it's only early afternoon and we both feel OK we decide to press on for Bidarray. After another hour or so we come to a point of steep descent which Douggie describes as 'one of the narrowest and most vertigo-inspiring' on the whole GR10 – in other words, keep a clean pair of pants handy. We wonder if 'vertigo-inspiring' is a good or a bad thing and Rob then goes on to read that this particular section has 'caused more than its fair share of injuries'. Well, these words of wisdom aren't really helping, so we decide to take a break and have a bit of lunch before we launch ourselves off into oblivion. We tuck into bread, cheese, chorizo and a few dates, and then treat ourselves to a bit of chocolate. These little breaks are great: the feeling of satisfaction after a few hours of walking and the real pleasure and strength gained from such a simple meal. We lie back in the grass, the gentle breeze and warm sun on our faces, and soak up our luxurious surroundings: the space, silence and freshness of the mountain air.

Then we prepare for the treacherous descent, picking our way down. From here we can see that it is indeed a steep drop, the path falling dramatically away down into a wooded valley towards the town of Bidarray. Great shattered boulders of rock and stone cover the hillside, indication of some serious land movement long ago, and the path has to wind its narrow way through this prehistoric obstacle course. Actually, it's not that bad, either in a vertiginous way or an ankle-breaking way, though we do have to concentrate as we cautiously walk, clamber and stumble. The trail is very rocky and steep at times and makes for slow progress as we step or jump from stone to stone, twisting and turning as we go. If anything it's my knees that feel the strain with the constant downward jarring motion, and Rob opens up a lead ahead of me. Rob seems a lot less cautious, throwing himself downhill with a fair bit of slipping, sliding and falling over on the way. He's a bit like a weird kind of rubber man, I think to myself briefly.

As we reach the last stages of the descent we see a sign for the Grotte du Saint qui Sue (Saint Sue?) and can't resist a little detour to take a look, partial as we both are to a good *grotte*. In the end we can't find it, or aren't looking hard enough, and haven't got the energy to veer too far from the beaten track. It takes close to two hours to finish the descent, which ends with a pleasant drop down into a river valley – but just when we begin to think we are nearly there we start to climb again and have a final hour-long exhausting climb up to the village of Bidarray. It seems to take an eternity to find the *gîte d'étape*. It's amazing how the last half hour of the day's walk can seem so hard after the previous seven or eight hours, but it's the anticipation of reaching the end that makes it so difficult.

The man running the place is a very cool, good-looking kind of guy. I don't know about Rob but he makes me feel a little inadequate. He has a sort of knowing smile on his face, as if we might be figures of fun in some kind of strange way, although equally this could simply be my own sense of insecure paranoia. The gîte seems to operate as an outward bound centre and there are some young people hanging around outside chatting. We book ourselves in and, having spotted the Scottish couple gingerly picking their way down the trail earlier, let the guy know that two more stragglers are on their way. He shows us to our bunks and we discover we are in a little cosy room for four; he clearly thinks we and the Scots are part of the same group. Too tired to argue, we slip out and get some food from the shop just down the road and Rob cooks another superb meal of pasta and chorizo. The gîte guy then shows us all this food left in the fridge from a previous group that needs to be used up, so we tuck into that as well. Fed and watered we saunter down the road, past a large *fronton* and find a nice-looking bar for a few beers. Bidarray is a nice place – not quite a town but larger than a village. Strangely, it is split into two parts, so we don't get to see the whole place, but it certainly gets the thumbs-up from both of us and we feel good as we settle into a beer with the church bells going off around us. In fact, it's here that we first realise that for some reason the church bells in these parts always sound the hour twice, as if once wasn't enough. Now don't get me wrong, the sound of the church bells ringing in a Pyrenean village is sublime indeed, but when you get to the end of the evening (or first thing in the morning for that matter) that's a hell of a lot of bell action going on.

In the bar, Rob catches the waitress' eye and he increases his French vocabulary by asking for a *cendrier* (ashtray). As we sit in the garden our Scottish friends come along and join us and we finally get around to introducing ourselves. They are Craig and Lucy and, bizarrely, we discover that they live just a few miles away from us back home. Craig is a jovial character with a mischievous face and good sense of humour, whilst Lucy makes little asides to herself in an amusing and very engaging manner. I guess they are in their mid to late thirties; Craig medium build and bald-headed with an infectious grin and Lucy dark-haired and attractive. Whilst we talk, the well-groomed French woman walks past and we say hello. She has met up with her husband and obviously got to Bidarray some time before we did, so we assume she must be a very fast walker or is travelling by more than just her feet. Craig and Lucy, continuing their gastronomic tour of the GR10, decide to eat in the restaurant inside, emerging later clutching their stomachs and bemoaning the amount of food they had to negotiate.

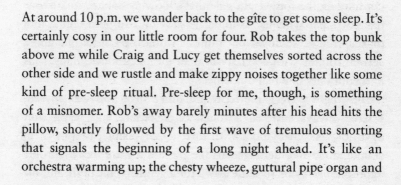

At around 10 p.m. we wander back to the gîte to get some sleep. It's certainly cosy in our little room for four. Rob takes the top bunk above me while Craig and Lucy get themselves sorted across the other side and we rustle and make zippy noises together like some kind of pre-sleep ritual. Pre-sleep for me, though, is something of a misnomer. Rob's away barely minutes after his head hits the pillow, shortly followed by the first wave of tremulous snorting that signals the beginning of a long night ahead. It's like an orchestra warming up; the chesty wheeze, guttural pipe organ and nasal trumpeting slowly but relentlessly building up into a mighty crescendo, a cacophony of wind and mucous that rips through the room like a twister. For a moment you are in the eye of the storm, an all-too-short oasis of stillness and eerie quiet before inevitably the nose piccolo gently whistles the introduction to a new movement that once again rises up and crashes down with a clap of sonorous thunder.

I find myself swallowing at key moments, as Rob's own phlegm rises, and reluctantly find myself attempting to anticipate the swell, riding the waves of snorts and shudders. And with the snoring, Rob also hurls himself around the bed like a somnambulistic Greco-Roman wrestler, sending shudders and creaks through the timbers of the bunk, which gives me the feeling of being deep in the bowels of some disease-ridden eighteenth-century vessel ploughing across the wild Atlantic.

Some time later, it's hard to know exactly when, Rob is joined by new snoring; a deep and regular ebb and flow, which, if anything, reminds me more of the monotonous deep-toned hum of a cross channel ferry than Fitzroy and his creaking *Beagle*. I think it must be Lucy and this is then confirmed when I hear Craig shoving her and telling her to keep quiet because it might wake us up. Well, I admire Craig's consideration but it's a touch misplaced considering the force-eight gale that's blowing in the bunk above me. I wonder whether I should be shoving Rob and telling him to keep the noise down but think it would be a little like going several rounds with a grizzly bear in the pitch black; dangerous and with only one real outcome.

You might have gathered that I don't sleep too well myself. I have always suffered a touch of insomnia and being shut in a hot, darkened room with three other people, two of them sounding off like deranged truffle pigs, is a little like a chronic agoraphobic trying to settle down for a gentle picnic in the middle of Hampstead Heath on a sunny Sunday afternoon. I have the trekkers' insomniac survival kit spread around me – water, two torches, book, paper and pen – but I get myself into a bit of state in the dark trying to find what's what. I try writing up my journal but am conscious of the light from my torch waking people up and it's hard to get right inside my sleeping bag. My book has slipped down the side of the bed and is unreachable and as I try to take a swig of water I send my metal water bottle clattering across the floor, which causes all the snoring to momentarily pause. I think about getting up but worry about being discovered wandering around the gîte naked in the middle of the night. So I lie there, staring into the darkness, knowing at some time sleep will eventually get hold of me. At some point I hear Craig and Lucy muttering to each other and then they both mysteriously leave the room and don't come back. I wonder if they have been driven out by Rob's or my own night-rustling activity. Still, it's given me something to think about for a while.

DAY 5

BIDARRAY TO ST-ÉTIENNE-DE-BAÏGORRY

After my two or three hours' sleep I wake up feeling pretty fragile and give Rob a shove to stir him into action. Not only do I sleep terribly but I naturally wake up very early as well, so I seem to have taken on the role of human alarm clock. The mornings, even at this early stage, are falling into a pattern of being a bit of a low-point as we both feel crap and take a while to get into the rhythm of the day. Rob tells me that he always sleeps terribly and I guess with all his thrashing around his sleep is about as much disturbed as mine is absent. Also, with much amusement, he christens me 'The Hamster' due to my noisy nocturnal activities (he was clearly more awake than I thought). He says that all he could think about was the idea of me scampering around on my little wheel and 'hamstering' about in my little paper-filled nest. I tell him that 'hamstering' isn't a word but he says it is now. Craig and Lucy have left already and I tell Rob about them sneaking out of the room in the night. He reckons they must have gone for 'a quick one', which I suppose is possible, and we wonder where the act itself may have taken place. Actually, Craig later tells us that Lucy was feeling unwell and she went out to throw up.

Down at breakfast Cool Gîte Man is calmly running the show and he tells me where to find today's food – the usual bread and jam but this time with an option of a few cereals. I am downstairs before Rob and while I sit at the table drinking coffee Cool Gîte Man comes over a makes a crack about 'ze Ingleesh' and how we would probably like to have 'ze fool Ingleesh brakefoost'. I humour him and say 'Yes, that would be lovely', but feel annoyed by what seems to be his gentle mockery. Five minutes later, as I sit nursing my coffee and wounded pride, he returns with a glorious plate of scrambled egg and bacon and I feel a little ashamed of my casual mistrust. Rob comes down and is amazed to see me tucking into 'ze fool Ingleesh' and manages to get our man to knock one up for him as well.

Feeling much better and revived by the caffeine we get Douggie and the map out and have a look at the day's walk. Today it looks like a really tough eight-hour 14-km walk with a climb of over 1,000 m. Douggie warns us that there is only one place to get water along the way so we stock up with a couple of extra litres – as if we needed any extra weight. I check the time and realise my watch has broken and so I throw it in the bin. I guess that makes me about half an ounce lighter, anyway.

We load up and head off, and for the first hour or so the footpath gently winds away from the village and up the hillside. However, it soon becomes pretty steep and we can tell it's going to be a scorcher of a day. As I walk, though, my legs actually begin to feel pretty good and I find myself stretching out and hitting a good rhythm as we head upwards. After a couple of hours we reach the

Pic d'Iparla and have climbed over 1,000 m. We are knackered and stop to rest for a bit and chew on a few dates, washed down with our precious water. From here the GR10 runs along the ridge of Crête d'Iparla and the views are stunning. To our left the ridge falls away dramatically, creating an immense open vista with spectacular views across to Spain. Vultures circle effortlessly and we also see a couple of lonesome eagles, although we can't be sure of their exact type. A couple of people along the way state with some authority that they are golden eagles, which we are happy to believe. As we walk I really feel that this is what I had fantasised: the incredible open space, the vastness of our surroundings and the clarity of the mountain air. It's definitely the best day so far and we are both in awe of the scenery.

We take several short breaks as we go and I suffer from my first attack of Welting Bum Crack, a nasty sweat-induced chaffing of the inner buttock area resulting in large red welts. I wish I had brought some snugly fitting underwear rather than my loose boxers, because whilst the airy freedom of movement is rather nice, the combination of sweat, friction, bollocks and buttocks is definitely not. I drag out the medical kit from the bottom of my rucksack and apply a bit of aqueous cream, with Rob's advice. I ask him if he fancies applying it for me but he turns me down politely. The other problem with the loose boxers is that insects can fly up my shorts with ease and do a little dance around my nether regions. I make a mental note to ask Nicky to send some over some decent pants when we get to Luchon.

We drop down to the Col d'Harrieta and enter a large wood of beech trees that provide a welcome respite from the heat of the sun, but then have to make another steep climb up to Pic Buztanzelhay and we are getting seriously hot and exhausted. Our water is eked out carefully and it is amazing how precious it becomes and how a simple glug is like manna from heaven. The going is tricky too and we pick our way over rocks and stones, having to concentrate on every step. It's easy to see how one could drift off and take a nasty tumble. We then hit the steep 1,000-m descent and I struggle with the stress it puts on my knees. The descent goes on forever and I find it much harder than the climbing – Rob bounds down gazelle-like and waits patiently for me to catch up. We walk through a pleasant bit of woodland and sit on a tree trunk for a little snack of chocolate and figs. As we quietly contemplate our progress it suddenly begins to rain, a few drops gradually building up to what feels like a potential downpour. We look at each and without saying a word simultaneously reach for our ponchos, but as we do so the rain stops suddenly, our arms frozen in the air, mid-movement. It's a true comedy moment and we laugh loud and long, perhaps a little too hysterically. It's a welcome little interlude in a gruelling day but we soon continue downwards and eventually reach the outskirts of the town.

All our water is finished and we are both gasping for a drink. We must look like we need it because as we pass by a small house the owner beckons us over and lets us fill up our bottles from his outside tap. This is my first true test of drinking local water without checking out whether it is 'potable' but what the hell, I'm too desperate to be choosy so we fill up and then take some well-needed swigs. I've always been overly cautious about drinking water when 'abroad' (or obsessively paranoid, Nicky might say, and Rob also mocks me deservedly for my middle-class, suburban anxieties) so for me this is a small but significantly watery step in the right direction.

A bit further along the route my phone goes off and it's my daughter Jess, miraculously on the other end. It's amazing to hear her voice; I feel a little overwhelmed and the pain of missing her hits me like a blow to the stomach. Strangely, it's hard to know what to say; I want to tell her how much I love her and want to hug her but it's hard to convey how I truly feel, so I tell her about the 'enormous mountain' we have just climbed down from and we chat about little things. Hanging up is terrible, like an execution, and I feel myself sliding into a pit of misery compounded by physical exhaustion and knees that feel like they are about to shatter. The last half hour's walking is a real killer, made worse by the anticipation of the day's finish and the fact that once again we can't find the bloody gîte. Douggie's little hand-drawn maps, whilst very fetching, are pretty useless and we curse them vehemently.

We don't really get to see much of the town but it is clearly a working agricultural kind of place and apparently has a strong history as a productive and at times very well-off farming town, being the market centre of the Vallée des Aldudes (great name... Dude Valley?). As well as being known for its ham, preserved mushrooms and our own particular favourite, *brebis* cheese, the town also produces the local Irouléguy wines, which for many years were the only appellation red and rosé produced in the Pays Basque.

Eventually, at around 6.30 p.m. and after over ten hours' walking we finally find the gîte and stagger in, slipping our rucksacks gratefully off our backs and onto the floor. It's deserted, and after looking around for a bit we find the owner, a fairly rough-and-ready but genial man who shows us the ropes and tells us the supermarket is closing in about ten minutes. It's my turn to cook and unfortunately this also means buying the prerequisite materials, so before I've had a chance to sit down and gather my breath I have to leg it down the road to get to the shop before it closes. I go the wrong way at first and have to double back, but just make it as they are beginning to close and manage to get a couple of cans of cassoulet and some bread and beer. The cassoulet, although cheap and cheerful, is very tasty and satisfyingly filling. Haricot beans in tomato sauce with sausage and bacon, mopped up with fresh bread and washed down with cold lager. Superb.

The gîte is a big place with a well-equipped functional kitchen and a good large garden that apparently you can camp in for a princely sum of €3 per person. The cost of a bed is only €10 and all in all these places are remarkably good value. So far they all seem very different in size, atmosphere and facilities and there is an enjoyable surprise factor in not quite knowing what kind of place we will be walking into. Like this one, the gîtes often seem to be located on the outskirts of the town, not unlike many youth hostels back in Britain, but that suits as fine as apart from tonight's mad dash to the supermarket we are generally too knackered to be going too far after a day on the trail.

We discover there is one other couple staying (not to say that Rob and I necessarily qualify as being a 'couple'); some nice French folks who are walking a week's section of the GR10. There's no sign of Craig and Lucy so we assume that they are staying in the posh hotel in the main part of the village, no doubt tucking into the *menu gastronomique*. We chat for a bit and sit outside to eat, knocking back the last of the beer, and gradually we begin to recover from the day's walking. I still feel totally shattered though, physically and emotionally, and actually quite depressed. The acute sadness and homesickness I felt after speaking to Jess is building to the point where I start to think about giving up the walk. Would it be such a terrible thing, to simply call it a day and catch a train back home? The idea is seductive, but the fear of failure also drives me and I find myself caught up in the conflict somewhere in between. I wonder about voicing some of my doubts to Rob, but it seems that somehow our capacity to complete this challenge depends partly upon us each being able to bolster the other's confidence, to coax each other along, and I don't want to sow any seeds of doubt or failure after just the first few days. Both of us are masters of self-doubt; it's the one area in which we both excel, so I choose to remain silent, although I've no doubt that Rob picks up that I am feeling very low.

The French couple have their own room at the end of one of the dorms, which are set out on two levels, sleeping all in all about forty or fifty people. It's a big space so we take a floor each, both enjoying the sense of personal space. I write my journal and draw a picture of Jess and me next to each other. In the picture, there are tears running down my face.

DAY 6

ST-ÉTIENNE-DE-BAÏGORRY
TO ST-JEAN-PIED-DE-PORT

Aching, tired, knees sore, I am generally feeling miserable and unprepared for the day's walking ahead – so what's new? It's about a six-hour schedule today with what looks like a lot of road walking, which is something of a mixed blessing. I feel worried about my knees after yesterday's painful descent and think that perhaps road walking might be less aggravating, although I also know that mile after mile of walking on hot, hard tarmac can bring its own problems. The glimmer on the otherwise rather troubled horizon is that tomorrow is our first rest day and the thought of a day off in St-Jean-Pied-de-Port spurs us on. We finish off last night's cassoulet for breakfast and wash it down with tea and bread. The nice French couple we chatted to a little last night are already preparing to set off. Apparently, the gîte owner has said that there is danger of thunderstorms today, perhaps later in the afternoon, so we have a short tête-à-tête about whether to stick to the trail or take the main road to St-Jean-Pied-de-Port, to avoid the possibility of being caught out in a storm. We come to the conclusion that it looks OK and that we should be up and over the top before the weather turns.

The climb is a considerable 860 m and overall isn't too bad – walking uphill and on the flat is merciful to my knees. We decide to skip the optional climb over the peak, Monhoa, partly because of the weather but also because we can't be bothered. However, it has to be said that Rob is always keener and more enthusiastic than me when it comes to an optional peak or a possible HRP variant – that's the 'Haute Randonnée Pyrénéene' alternative to the GR10 that stays high up on the ridge – and his eagerness for a challenge puts me to shame. I am aware that I am avoiding any extra mileage that might make my knees worse. But we can't avoid eventually walking downhill and the final descent kills me, every jarring step making me wince with pain. It's a shame because as we descend into the valley the sight of St-Jean-Pied-de-Port in the distance, nestling amongst the green hills, is beautiful and would have been cherished under different circumstances. The weather is close and sweaty and apart from a few distant rumbles there has been no sign of the threatened storm. The last couple of hours into town prove to be a gruelling slog on the hard, baking road in the mid-afternoon heat and I can feel my feet beginning to do strange things. This is our first experience of a condition that we christen 'pancake foot': a condition of the foot caused by excessive and sustained pounding on hot and hard tarmac road, leading to a general flattening of the overall foot structure with associated numbness, tingling and stabbing pains across the toes.

As we eventually approach the town we consult Douggie about the accommodation situation. We have two options and pass by the more obvious in favour of a gîte in the old part of the town that our trusty guide says is run by a marvellously hospitable Dutch woman. He neglected to mention that it is a pilgrim lodge. St-Jean-Pied-de-Port provides a crossing point for the GR10 and 'El

Camino de Santiago', the great 'Way of St James' pilgrimage route that leads people from all corners of the world across France, over the Pyrenees and to the cathedral of Santiago de Compostela in Galicia in north-west Spain, and ultimately for some to Cape Finisterre on the Atlantic coast. Now, I don't know about the pilgrimage but I would go to Finisterre purely on the basis of its hallowed place in the shipping forecast, which has many a time sent me floating off into a peaceful slumber. I recommend it for any fellow insomniacs.

The town itself sits at the base of the Ronceveaux Pass across the Pyrenees – 'Pied-de-Port' meaning at the 'foot of the pass' – and for this reason is something of a gathering place for the pilgrims on the Way of St James before they stride across the mountains. It's a beautiful old walled town, centred around the gorgeously cobbled *rue de la citadelle* that leads from the fifteenth-century Porte St Jacques down to the Porte d'Espagne, the old city gate that sits by the bridge over the river Nive. High up on the hill above and throwing an impressively protective arm around the shoulders of this lovely place is the citadel, which was given a serious makeover in the seventeenth century by Vauban, the prodigious military engineer who left his fortified fingerprints over much of France.

We find the gîte, which is in fact very pleasantly located halfway up the aforementioned *rue de la citadelle* that leads steeply down to the river and the main part of town. Our Dutch host is indeed very hospitable but seems to regard us with a slight air of suspicion as we explain that we are not actually pilgrims but simple GR10ers looking for a place to stay. Still, she seems reassured and informs us of the rules, which amongst others include a 10 p.m. curfew and the requirement to be up at 8 a.m. so that the room can be cleaned – no lie-in then. Rob and I exchange questioning looks; was this quite what we had planned for our rest day? There is a somewhat austere and, let's face it, rather Christian quality to the place, but it also has a welcoming ambience. We both clock the guitar hanging on the wall, which is enough for us to take the plunge and book for two nights. Rob and I both like to play guitar and have spent many an evening around a dinner table or campfire playing together and singing songs, although to be fair I tend to leave the singing to Rob as he has a lovely voice. I don't know about Rob, but I get withdrawal symptoms when deprived of a musical instrument for too long (restless, twitchy, tapping of fingers on inanimate objects, etc.) and so the fact that our rest day coincides with the possible availability of a guitar is a welcome thought.

After the usual showering and washing of socks, pants and shirts (my turn) we head out to see the town. We have a number of things on our 'to do and buy' list, including painkillers, knee supports, ear plugs, insoles and tracking down the sole Internet cafe, but come to the conclusion that our first priority is a cold beer to celebrate our first week on the road. Of course, one thing leads to another and we find ourselves holed up in a cosy little place for the rest of the afternoon and evening. After the mandatory thirst-quenching beer we get through a litre of the local red and then move on to warming hot chocolate before ordering some food and more wine. I go for the paella and Rob goes for the Basque chicken and we descend into a food-and-alcohol-sustained stupor that staves off the exhaustion of the day's walking. The two attractive waitresses running the bar keep us captivated with their exquisite and rather French portrayal of efficiency and boredom, and whilst in our wine-fuelled fantasy we think that they are rather taken with us two rugged English adventurers the reality is probably something more of a polite tolerance. Still, they humour us, writing down the names of songs on the radio for Rob, who is compiling a list of obscure Euro music, and indulge us in our feeble attempts at conversation.

There is something uniquely captivating about sitting in a bar like this for six-plus hours, idly chatting, drinking and observing. A hundred little dramas get played out: the delivery guy on the moped who gets more than the expected peck on each cheek from the waitress; the anxious guy in the corner, chain-smoking and hunched over his laptop; the ebb and flow of customers who wash around us while we remain rooted to our table; the tooting cars, friendly waves and shouted greetings of passing neighbours and the rich smells of pastry, coffee and tobacco that float in from the street. I feel seduced by this rich tapestry and immerse myself in it like a warm bath on a cold winter's day.

Eventually we stagger out into the evening light and on the way back to the gîte get tempted in somewhere for a final couple of beers. Tomorrow is a rest day, after all. As we finally walk up the cobbled street to the gîte we congratulate ourselves for making it back in time for the 10.30 p.m. curfew, although our bonhomie is short-lived when we find the lights out and the door firmly bolted. With a guilty pang of mutual realisation it dawns on us that our hostess did indeed say 10 p.m. Shit. Shut out of a pilgrim lodge. We both glance up at the building in hope of finding some kind of salvation and see a large pub-like painted sign hanging from the wall. It has a picture of a cockerel on it and simply says in large letters 'Le Coque'. Well, that does it for us and we descend into fits of laughter. Not just any laughter but full blown, uncontrolled hysteria; the kind of hysteria that involves squeaking, hooting, tears and that funny suppressed throaty thing. The more we try and stop the worse it gets, and when we think we have it under control one glance at the sign sets us off again. People cross over to the other side of the street to pass us by, which, under the circumstances, is probably about as fitting a version of the Good Samaritan as we deserve. Eventually, the hysteria subsides and we wipe our eyes dry and pluck up the courage to knock on the door. A light goes on in a small window not far above our heads and our Dutch Madame briskly pops out her head and then quickly disappears from view. We realise that being so close she must have heard everything and we begin to feel a little ashamed of ourselves. With a clunk and rattle of bolts being drawn the door opens and we are ushered in, heads hung low and mumbling pathetic apologies. She simply says, 'Well, you're in now.'

DAY 7

ST-JEAN-PIED-DE-PORT – REST DAY

Woken up by the usual morning dormitory sounds of people rustling around in plastic bags and ferreting about in their rucksacks, I realise I seem to have slept pretty well, and can't remember being disturbed by any snoring from the Robster, or anyone else for that matter. After stumbling around for an hour or so we head out and wander around town in a slightly dazed state, looking for somewhere to have breakfast. My knees are incredibly sore and I am really starting to wonder if I can continue with the walk. After coffee and croissants, I buy knee supports at the pharmacy and a two-week supply of Nurofen and hope for the best. I also buy some earplugs, which turn out to be one of my better purchases of the trip.

We find the Internet cafe, although I use the term in its loosest sense. It is in fact just one computer in a broom cupboard in a small bar by the train station. It is also next to the toilet, so at regular intervals someone bursts in fumbling with their trousers, takes one look at me and beats a hasty retreat. So what's new? I wait in anticipation for a particularly desperate person to crash in through the door and piss all over the computer. In my hungover state it takes me about half an hour to find my emails and my confusion is not helped by the fact that on a French keyboard you have to crack a top-secret encrypted code in order to find the @ symbol. I fail the test miserably and rather embarrassingly have to go and ask the barman for help.

After getting in a bit more shopping and also, with a flash of inspiration from Rob, some new spongy insoles that might help to stave off further attacks of pancake foot, we head back to our holy gîte for a few hours of rest and relaxation. It is, in fact, very pleasant and we sit in the sun in the terraced garden playing guitar and ukulele. I think we also do a reasonable job at entertaining the few souls knocking around, and even our Dutch Madame seems to be warming to us after last night's debacle.

I go up to the dorm for an afternoon nap and when I wander back down I find Rob squeezed between two attractive and very posh young women. Not just posh totty, but posh pilgrim totty. Rob chats to them both effortlessly, charming them with his easy wit and gentle humour, but I find myself a little overwhelmed by their evangelical spirit. The gîte is starting to fill up as more pilgrims arrive after their day on the road and the place is buzzing with their chatter and laughter and general goodwill. They excitably exchange stories about their adventures along the way; they compare their pilgrim passports that get stamped at certain points along the route; they hug, kiss, embrace and I'm sorry to say I find the whole thing overbearing and somewhat uncomfortable. Don't get me wrong; this is about me, not them. As a fundamental atheist I tend to feel ill-at-ease in the company of hard core believers of any faith, but what really gets me is that this lot are just too damn cheerful; full of that evangelical zeal that in my experience Americans are often so good at. Later on I chat to Rob about it and I come to the conclusion that in fact I rather envy their happiness and energy and expressions of comradeship. They seem to almost physically sparkle with exuberance and just a little of that would do me nicely; and of course, the fact that I envy them and want to be like them just makes me feel more uncomfortable. We conclude that I'm really pretty shallow and pathetic. Rob, being perhaps more open-minded on spiritual matters, has no problem with the situation, except perhaps the problem of controlling his carnal urges.

For dinner, we join in with the big communal meal which begins with a minute's silence from our Madame. She then blesses 'El Camino de Santiago' and rather touchingly adds on a little extra blessing for the two pilgrims of the GR10. The meal itself is excellent, although I continue to struggle with the whole group experience thing. For one whose personal motto is 'Hell is other people' I manage the social chit-chat as best I can. I do, however, have a good talk with a nice Dutch guy who is also suffering with a bad knee and he gives me some useful tips as to how to walk down hills. Strangely, his advice is to not walk at all down the hills but instead employ a gentle, small-stepped running gait, which he then proceeds to demonstrate a number of times. I think he hasn't quite taken on board the fact that I am carrying nearer to 20 kg (compared to his humble satchel) and that the 'hills' of the GR10 are a little bigger than his puny pilgrim ones (they stick to the flat as much as possible until the mountains and, let's face it, they go over them whilst we are going along them). Actually, this is unfair. St-Jean-Pied-de-Port to Santiago de Compostela is a seriously long walk, let alone the fact that many of these folks have walked a long way just to get here, so hats off to them. Anyway, I feel much encouraged by my friend's advice and after a couple more glasses of wine I down some Nurofen and hit the sack.

It's been good to have a rest day, or recovery day as it might better be called, and whilst we both feel very satisfied with having got through the first week I do feel a certain degree of apprehension about the days ahead and my dodgy knees. But whilst it has been a tough and very physically demanding week we are pleased to have got this far and when we look at the map we can see that St-Jean-Pied-de-Port actually looks a considerable distance from our start point of Hendaye all those days ago. I don't know how far we have actually walked so far but blimey... it looks impressive on the map. Also looking quite impressive at the moment is my beard, which although in its early stages of development is just starting to take its first few baby steps towards full maturity. Quite why I am using the metaphor of child development to describe my beard is beyond me. Whatever next? Will my beard reach its hairy adolescent stage and start rebelling against me before gradually conforming and applying for a degree in geography. Whatever, it is at that somewhat itchy, scratchy, irritating stage... oh hang on, that is adolescence! Rob's beard grows twice as fast as mine (is he twice the man I am?) and so his looks fully mature already. By the time we get to Banyuls he is going to look like Brian Blessed.

DAY 8

ST-JEAN-PIED-DE-PORT
TO PHAGALCETTE

I reluctantly half-open my eyes and cautiously survey the situation. I suddenly remember I am in a room full of pilgrims and immediately look for the earnest expressions in their faces. I hate these mornings, when other people are rustling around and faffing about with their boots, bags and assorted walking paraphernalia and generally rummaging around amongst their nether regions. My strategy is to avoid eye-contact and say as little as possible. Rob is asleep but looks as if he has been dreaming in the night that his mattress was an alligator. I give him a shove, which he acknowledges with a mournful sigh, and then go about the business of the morning ablutions, which again is no easy thing in these bunkhouse situations. People sit on the edge of their beds pretending to be noisily stuffing something important into a plastic bag, when really they are waiting to hear the click of a lock that signals that the toilet or shower is free and then whoosh – in a flash they're gone. So much for any displays of patience and saintly calm that I half expected from my pilgrim comrades; and inwardly I admonish myself for even thinking that pilgrims might not need to shit, shave and shower like the rest of us mere mortals.

Down at breakfast we tuck into, just for a change, a feast of dried toast and jam washed down with warm coffee, and I slip on my knee-supports and dose myself up with Nurofen. Our clothes are still damp so we tie them onto the back of our rucksacks to dry in the sun and we begin to resemble mobile launderettes. We pay our €10 each (a bargain compared to the 30 or 40 it would cost to stay in a hotel) and say goodbye to our hostess, who I think has truly forgiven us for our misdemeanours a couple of nights ago – all in all it has proved to be a good resting place. Thankfully, it only looks like a four- or five-hour walk to Phagalcette, with a lowly climb of around 550 m, and the beginning stretch is a remarkably pleasant stroll on good roads along some very gently rolling countryside. In a way, it reminds me of Sussex and I start seeing houses that I would like to buy; it's a place that I would like to live. It may be the double dose of Nurofen, or maybe even our brush with the pilgrims, but I actually start to feel quite content and even my knees are feeling a little better.

As we walk, Rob confesses that he had half hoped one of the pilgrim girls might have slipped into his bed in the middle of the night and we spend some time discussing whether I would have been more disturbed by the sound of him snoring or having sex.

We stop for a rest in the village of Estérencuby that marks the beginning of the climb up to the gîte. It's a small village with a bar and large hotel and the mandatory *fronton* that appears out of scale; the place seems pretty much deserted and just a little desolate. It must be lunchtime. The bar is closed so I head into the hotel and manage to rustle up a couple of cold Cokes that go down well. We are both in something of an introspective mood and we touch gently upon issues of depression, loneliness, relationships and the general phenomenon that is male existential angst. This isn't the subject matter that men generally engage in too easily, and to be fair it is only a matter of twenty minutes or so before we move on to talking about pilgrim's breasts and the texture of our last bowel movement. But I am aware that Rob seems quite low, as I was a few days ago in St Étienne, and again it seems like we're taking these dips in mood in turn, so that we can give each other a little hand up when we need to. No doubt the time will come when we both simultaneously descend into our emotional pit of doom but then, I think, the trick with this adventure is to just keep walking. If in doubt just put one foot in front of the other and keep walking. Simple.

We could have stayed in Estérencuby but agree, as planned, to carry on up the hill to Phagalcette. It's still early and this will save us a couple of hours and a 500-m climb tomorrow. The walking is good and my knees feel much better when going uphill, although I start to dread any downhill sections of the trail. This isn't a good sign, as my guess is there is going to be as much downward stuff as upward stuff over the next seven weeks, that being the nature of mountains, but it's an unexpected turnaround to find myself dreading walking downhill. The scenery is superb: green, flower-drenched meadows, rolling hills and ahead of us some serious mountains that ripple in the heat of the summer air. It really starts to feel as if we are moving into a new phase of the walk as we slowly head towards the higher region of the central Pyrenees. We stop for a lunch of bread, cheese and chocolate and from the field of lush grass in which we are lying get a lovely view of the valley stretching back along our route towards the red roofs of St-Jean-Pied-de-Port.

After about two and half hours, and with the help of Douggie, we find the little *gîte d'étape*, called Kaskoleta, and as we amble into the front garden we are greeted by Craig and Lucy, who acknowledge our arrival with friendly hoots, jeers and laughter. It seems our paths are destined to cross but it is good to see them, a bit of much-needed camaraderie to break up the long hours of walking during the day. That's not to say of course that Rob's company is anything but welcome, indeed I count myself lucky to have him as a friend and companion, but there is also an intensity about spending so much of one's waking (and sleeping) hours with one other person and my guess is that we both welcome a bit of varied social interaction.

Also in residence, sitting coolly drinking coffee, is the well-groomed and super speedy French lady from our earlier stop, who apparently arrived well ahead of all of us. She looks like she has just been dropped in by helicopter after a quick shopping trip in central Paris. Brigit, as we discover she is called, is a truly formidable woman: she must be perhaps in her early fifties and puts the rest of us to shame with her steadfast pace and ability to turn mountain trekking in something of a chic pastime. We learn she is from Toulouse and whilst her English is sporadic we manage to get by with much waving of arms and strange gesticulating. What with Brigit and Craig and Lucy it seems we have started to become a little band of GR10ers, bonded by the route, and we name our group captain 'Brigit of Toulouse'. That said, we almost hear Craig and Lucy's hearts sink when they learn that we are in the same cosy dorm for the night. Hooray... another night with 'Snorer and Hamster'.

The gîte itself is a real gem, small, comfortable and superbly located on the edge of the hillside, and we sit outside for an hour or so chatting, playing the ukulele and taking in the views across the valley. Rob has been diligently applying himself to the process of learning the ukulele, learning more chords by the day and adding new songs to his growing repertoire. His gentle voice and rhythmic strumming drift into the hazy air, sweet and pure, and it is a perfect accompaniment to the moment. It's a beautiful early evening, the warm sun casting an ambient glow upon the mountains. It is these moments, winding down after the day's walk and casually indulging in the scenic splendour of the Pyrenees, which make this journey so worthwhile. There is camaraderie between us, not just Rob and me but all of us as a group, and I feel like some kind of adventurer from another age as we forge ahead into unknown territory, powered only by the strength of our legs. Also, there is a real satisfaction that comes with the experience of physical exhaustion, a kind of earnest sense of self-worth that I rarely feel back home.

The evening meal is formidable: a gargantuan feast of pâté, ham, tomatoes, sausages, pasta, cheese and fruit – all washed down with some of the local brew, a rich and well-bodied red wine. The meal costs about €13 and you would be hard pushed to get better anywhere else; and with the cost of a bed only €12 it's superb value all round. I feel physically ill from eating so much and my stomach feels like it has swelled up to twice its normal size, which is pretty large at the best of times. Halfway through the meal another guy rolls up to eat, keeping his own counsel up at the far end of the table. We unimaginatively name him 'Camping Guy' as he is sleeping in his little one-man tent in the field outside. He is a mega-serious French man and has a haunted, slightly psychotic look about him, as if he is on the run after committing a particularly gruesome murder. He eats his food without muttering a word, apart from something about the weather, and retires to his tent. Up on the wall of the dining room is a huge and rather fierce-looking stuffed badger and Craig suggests we sneak outside and leave it at the entrance to Camping Guy's tent, but after much debate we decide against it on the grounds of personal safety.

DAY 9

PHAGALCETTE TO
CHALET D'IRATY

It was a bad night's sleep, mostly due to the large meal that sat like a dead weight in my stomach. After breakfast we get down to the pre-departure commotion of packing. Rob packs and unpacks his rucksack several times, something he seems to do most mornings now. Typically, he will pack it meticulously, making sure everything is in its right place and then, just when we are about to set off, realise that he needs something that is invariably squashed down in the very bottom, so he then has to unpack everything and repack it once more. I tend to just throw my stuff in haphazardly, hoping I can cram it all in. Rob laughs, though, when he sees me laboriously rolling up my sleeping bag and then try to squeeze it into the accompanying stuff bag. 'It's a stuff bag – you just stuff it in,' he says, after watching me do this for nearly a week now. Feeling foolish, I stuff it in. Ah, much easier.

Camping Man was the first to go; in fact no one saw him so he must have left at first light, probably hoping to get a good head start on the posse of *gendarmes* hot on his flaky heels. Brigit was second to go; looking pristine in her pressed trousers and freshly coiffed hair. She set off at a firm pace, clearly relishing the role of group leader although she is probably blissfully unaware of the high office we have assigned her. Next off are Craig and Lucy, who are reasonably organised in the mornings although there is much Scottish muttering as they head for the hills. Finally, after a last few delaying tactics to allow for the morning's ablutions we set off at around 8.30. I think about the trail we have left behind us: pots of jam, hats, bags of food and anything else we can jettison. Like Hansel and Gretel we could probably find our way back to Hendaye without the need of a map.

The walking is spectacular but a real killer. At one point, after an hour or so, we see Camping Man, Brigit and Craig and Lucy climbing up the hill on the other side of the valley, like a trail of little ants. All in all we have to climb about 1,800 m and although the ascent is split into a number of stages the going is really tough. We don't talk too much today, but for some reason I tell Rob a story about a man who lived in the village where I grew up, who had the tendency to use the phrase 'up your bum' all the time. I tell Rob that this bloke was probably, in my experience as a child-therapist, a 'raving paedo' and Rob replies that it seems as if everyone, in my experience as a child-therapist, is a 'raving paedo'. Rob, perhaps justifiably, questions my cynical world-view and suggests that there is *some* good in the world and that I might be looking at things through offender-coloured spectacles.

Furthermore, he counters that 'up your bum' might well be an affectionate northern expression, adding that he could remember his sister using it in the distant past. The unfortunate consequence of this erstwhile debate about the potential level of paedophilia in rural villages is that 'up your bum' has become the phrase of the day and echoes around the hills, along with several dodgy French translations. Later on Rob calls me a 'nobber' several times, which makes him chuckle no end. He assures me it is a term of endearment, but all I can respond with, predictably, is 'up your bum'.

As we make a slow descent down a valley we see Craig and Lucy one or two miles ahead of us, just about to start the big climb on the other side. Furthermore, from the luxury our position, from which we can see the path run up the hill opposite, we also see them miss the turning and head off in the wrong direction. We try shouting, but not too hard, and it is with a little glee that a short time later we get to the same point and then head up the trail ahead of them. We make fast progress and bomb up the hill: and while it is gruelling work we seem to have hit a good rhythm. These moments, although rare, feel amazing as somehow the body manages to organise itself into a complete walking machine and moves like clockwork. The motion is effortless and I can barely feel the rucksack on my back. I imagine my legs as hydraulic pistons, pumping and driving me up the steep inclines. God, if it could only always be like this. With an hour or so to go it begins to rain and we decide after some hesitation that it is a 'poncho moment' and go through the rather bizarre ritual of transforming each other into green Quasimodo-like apparitions. Still, once inside the poncho it feels quite good, as if I am sealed off from the outside world.

We push up to the Col d'Irau and then an incredibly steep section where there is no path as such but just markers leading us up a grassy hillside. Then from the top of this ridge we continue up a stony track that leads us to the high-point of the day, the Sommet d'Occabé which sits at 1,456 m. From here we begin to head downwards again, turning east along a well-used vehicle track and into a beech wood. The weather is deteriorating fast and it's amazing how conditions can turn on a sixpence in these parts. The rain brings with it a mist and gathering cloud that begins to wrap itself around us, cocooned as we are in our glistening green ponchos, and the rich smell of damp vegetation hangs in the air. It's lovely, in fact; the warm rain in a beech forest, the tap, tap, tap of the drops on the hood of my poncho and the lushness of the moss and lichen that mysteriously shrouds the trees. The carpet mulch of leaves underfoot is soft to walk on, making a pleasant change from the rocky path that we have had to pick our way through with care for so much of the day. Amazingly, a little further on, we overtake Brigit who is mightily impressed with our speed. She falteringly explains that she got lost a few times and Rob and I exchange a brief but knowing glance that acknowledges the possible historic shift in power that is taking place in this bedraggled area of French woodland.

After a total of close to eight hours of walking we eventually get to Chalet D'Iraty, which is in fact a ski resort, looking rather forlorn and dreary without the winter snow. We are surprised that we have got high enough to have reached ski-resort territory. The gîte here is a weird kind of domed igloo shape and reminds me of a chicken house or a large version of the metal pigsties I've seen out of the car window on the A303 near Stonehenge (some of you will know what I mean). We are totally drained, bedraggled and muddy as we burst into the office to get the key for our room and find out what to do.

We negotiate the shower and Rob cooks a delicious lentil and chorizo dish that could probably feed half the population of the Pyrenees. 'Just, like, to be on the safe side,' he says, heaving the bubbling cauldron of food onto the table. Craig and Lucy arrive about an hour after us looking like extras from *Night of the Living Dead*, as they hammer desperately on the glass door for us to let them in. They explain that they took a wrong turn and got lost and we nod compassionately. Another GR10er is also staying in the gîte, who we soon ascertain is called Corinne. Corinne is an attractive Parisienne in an Audrey Hepburn kind of way, with twinkling eyes and a beatific smile. She apparently left Hendaye the day after us, so she's done very well to get ahead. Rob does his best to engage her in his newly acquired French, his opening line naturally being 'Le sanglier est dans la bouilloire'. Corinne seems impressed and adds a little bird to the kettle and it seems like we are verging on some bizarre version of an old childhood game. I leave them to it and call Nicky and Jess and have a good chat. Again, the conversation feels difficult at times; it's hard to convey what I really feel and they compound my pangs of homesickness, but at the same time it is amazing to hear their voices. My knees have survived the day pretty well, probably because we were mainly going uphill, but I feel cold and fluey as if I might have a temperature.

At one point a man bursts in to the gîte in a whirlwind of energy and gusto and announces that he has just had a good meal up at the bar and is off to bed now. We wonder who the hell this bloke is and it turns out he is doing the hard core HRP trail and has 'dropped down' for the night to get supplies, a decent night's kip and to avoid a bit of dodgy weather up on high. He looks like some kind of superhero, all muscle and good cheer, and makes us GR10ers feel like pathetic wimps in comparison. He briefly whips out a 1:25-scale map to check his route for tomorrow about which Rob gets very excited and for a second I think that despite HRP Man's superhero physique Rob might try and wrestle him to the ground just to get his hands on the map. Anyway, after checking his route he bids us good night, adding that he won't see us in the morning, as he'll be gone by 5 a.m. HRP Man, our Pyrenean conquering hero. Of course, we all hate the bastard and quietly hope he breaks his legs as he leaps from peak to peak like Spider-Man.

Craig and Lucy are eating up at the resort bar/restaurant and we go up to join them and knock back a couple of hot chocolates each. Hot chocolate is quickly becoming our drink of choice; we seek solace in its warm comfort and energy from the sugar. Back at the ranch we retire for the night. Our room is tiny and consists of the cheapest, most fragile-looking bunk bed we have ever seen. Rob takes to the top and as the slats buckle under his weigh I fear the whole lot is going to come crashing down on top of me at any moment. Then, after a bit of journal writing, the light goes out and I prepare myself for a long night of lentil-induced methane poisoning.

DAY 10

CHALET D'IRATY TO LOGIBAR

Today we only have to walk about four hours and it is blissful to be able to have a lie-in and a good leisurely breakfast. The gîte is surrounded by goats and sheep with bells around their necks and as I lie half drifting in and out of sleep the sound is quite hypnotic. I listen carefully, tuning into each individual bell and picking out little patterns of sounds and rhythms amongst them. I actually slept reasonably well and feel content to let the others do their stuff and head out ahead of us. It's going to be downhill all the way today so I knock back my tabs of Nurofen and wonder if I could become addicted, seeing as I have been taking quite a lot over the last few days.

We decide to take an alternative route, suggested by Douggie, that initially follows the road and then veers off down some fields and an old cart track. Douggie warns us that there are no markers for this variation and that we may have to 'improvise', and consequently Rob enjoys taking us on every conceivable short cut, leading to a lot of clambering over fences, sliding down riverbanks and getting barked at by scary dogs. Rob is becoming increasingly unhappy about the 'useless' maps and starts going on about how we should have got 1:25s instead of 1:50s – and to be fair they are rubbish for these 'off-piste' sections when we are not following the main GR10 route. I feel slightly aggrieved and just a little defensive, since I spent nearly a hundred quid on them in Stanfords, the renowned London map and travel store, and the guy there assured me that most people seem to do fine with the 1:50s. Still, I appreciate that Rob likes orienteering and that the lack of detail on the maps must be frustrating, so can understand the odd 'map rant' here and there. Indeed, I am thankful that Rob has taken on the role of map-reader and general navigator, as I am pretty crap at this kind of stuff; but then I am also happy in my blissful ignorance to blindly follow the GR10 markers along the way and forgo the whole map thing, much to Rob's annoyance. I sense that the general map/route issue could become the source of a little conflict and feel cautious about where it might lead us, so to speak.

I am generally pretty hopeless at dealing with any form of conflict and tend to withdraw into myself, allowing resentment to bubble away uselessly. Rob, on the other hand, also doesn't like conflict but likes to deal with it openly and get it out of the way quickly. His is clearly the best method but I struggle to change my ways and I think Rob must be acutely aware of the times when I tend to drift off into my uneasy silence.

Possibly to prove the uselessness of the maps, Rob takes us on another short cut that takes us through a private farm, over a dodgy barbed wire fence and dangerously close to a massive bull, which eyes us with hostile suspicion. To top it all I tread in a huge pile of cow shit that laps over my treasured Berghaus boots, much to Rob's amusement. I ask him several times why we didn't just go the easy way, but I think he sees it all in the spirit of adventure and rather enjoys the merry dance he is taking me on.

For one reason or another, I find myself feeling quite fed up at times today and begin to retreat a little into my shell. I feel myself struggling with the social side of this whole experience. This is not to say that Rob isn't a treasured friend: this is much more about me and my need to be alone at times. As Nicky would testify, I am not exactly 'Mr Social' and at times it is a physical and mental effort to engage in what some might see as idle banter. Small talk is the worst; at a party or social gathering I am useless at making meaningless conversation for the sake of it, and generally just stare into the middle distance pretending I am thinking about something important or maybe looking at something interesting on the wall. While it's great to walk and chat with Rob, at times I need my peace and quiet and today is one of those days. Anyway, we emerge from our little cross-country diversion and stop for a rest and paddle in a nice stream, which feels great on the feet, and also say hello to some very nice pigs that are snouting around in someone's yard.

One advantage of this little GR10 variant is that it takes us through a village called Larrau, a pretty place with a cluster of white-washed, grey-roofed houses, where we stop for a beer in a lovely spot under a plane tree in the square. There is a little *épicerie* as well so we stock up on a few basics.

From here, it is only another half hour or so before we arrive in Logibar that essentially consists of just a single building, the Auberge Logibar, which houses a restaurant, gîte and what looks like a small hotel – and (as a special treat) table football. It's clearly a popular place though and there are quite a few day-trippers around who obviously use it as a base for exploring the area. All in all, there is a lot of commotion going on and it feels strange to have a little taste of the outside world. Craig and Lucy, Brigit and Corinne are in residence already, looking showered and relaxed, and the Scots give us a little cheer and a bit of kindly verbal abuse as we stroll in. It's my turn to cook and this time I take a risk with a chorizo risotto that actually turns out pretty well and I am pleased to note the envious looks from our comrades who have all bought a rather dodgy looking meal from the restaurant.

Chorizo seems to go with everything and along with *brebis* cheese provides a key part of our diet. For the uninitiated, chorizo is a dry-cured pork sausage flavoured to varying degrees with garlic and pimento (paprika), which gives it its distinctive red colour and strong, smoky flavour. Pyrenean chorizo has an especially strong spicy flavour and the beauty of this sausage is that when you cook with it the gorgeous smoky, spicy, garlic goodness oozes out and flavours whatever you might be cooking with it. And being a hard, dried sausage it is particularly suited to being stuffed in the pocket of my rucksack next to my tin whistle, ready for whatever occasion demands. We have a couple of beers and buy some postcards and then Rob (QPR) thrashes me (Man U) 4–0 at table football. The gîte is pretty basic, pretty much a bunkhouse with a raised platform upon which we line up in our sleeping bags like little larvae, waiting for the light of morning before we hatch out.

DAY 11

LOGIBAR TO ST ENGRÂCE

Today's stage looks pretty long, about 25 km and a climb of roughly around 1,000 m. As we drink our coffee and indulge in a chorizo omelette for breakfast (you see, chorizo with everything) we consult Douggie and discover that there is an alternative route that would take us over the 'spectacular Gorges D'Holzarte' and involve crossing an amazing-looking suspension bridge. We have seen pictures of this bridge in books and on postcards and although this variant will mean an extra couple of hours walking, Rob and I instantly agree that it's got to be done. The rest of the gang are taking the shorter route, and we score huge GR10 bonus points with our decision to take the long way round. Suited and booted and Vaselined to the hilt we set off, in the opposite direction to everyone else, for what feels like a bit of an adventure.

We both seem to be in a pretty good mood and physically in reasonable shape. I'm still on the Nurofen, but not quite as much and my knees seem to be getting better to the point that I am down to just the single knee support. I am astounded how well the supports work, like some kind of exoskeleton (sorry, too many Marvel comics as a child); but I still struggle with some of the steep descents, although uphill is no problem. So, strangely, I bound up the hills and Rob bounds down them. Rob complains of sore toes now and again but otherwise seems okay. He also continues to fall over quite a lot, which to be fair he seems quite content about. He explains that it is just the way he walks. Actually, I find it a little disconcerting, as I'm always half expecting him to go crashing to the ground at any moment and when he does I think he has injured himself in some way. His technique, when he slips and begins to go, is to twist around and land on his back, allowing his rucksack to take most of the blow. This also leaves him lying on his back waving his arms and legs in the air like an upended tortoise and me having to haul him back onto his feet.

I am not quite sure what Rob is made of; he seems impervious to damage and crashes around like a *sanglier*. I tentatively, and perhaps rather weedily, pick my way along the route and do anything to avoid taking a tumble, fearing that any kind of injury could wreck the whole journey. Another strange thing is that my back, which was causing me so many problems before we set out, is now absolutely fine, in fact better than fine. I think it must be because my rucksack is acting like some kind of brace and pulling my spine into a correct posture. Who'd have thought it? I make a note to tell my chiropractor when I get back; he seemed to be confident that I would be OK for the walk so maybe he knew more than I gave him credit for.

The trail is rocky but pretty well established and we still feel childishly pleased with ourselves for doing a 'variant', as Douggie puts it. We slowly climb and gain height above the gorge that we can glimpse below us, although the area is heavily wooded. After about forty-five minutes we see the suspension bridge in the distance, spanning the gorge and swaying disconcertingly. As we approach this somewhat dramatic scene set amidst the spectacular mountains, our conversation has for some reason moved on (again) to bodily functions and stories about past embarrassing mishaps. Rob tells me a story about something that happened in a supermarket in Bangkok and I tell him about a rather unpleasant bed-wetting experience in my younger days. I wonder, on reflection, if there is something about the symbolism of the gorge with its crevices and bowel-like depths that might have influenced this slight turn for the worse in our walking banter. The bridge is probably about 20 m across with wooden slats for the walkway itself and mesh railings to prevent one from tumbling over the edge into the gorge, the bottom of which must be at least 70–80 m below. Thick and reassuringly strong looking steel cables provide the suspension element of the bridge and at either end is a stone archway that lends to its overall dramatic appearance. The bridge is great fun and we muck around and take photos from various angles and try to scare each other out by shaking it around and trying to make it sway. This is as close as it gets to being Indiana Jones. Certainly, we are glad we made the effort.

The rest of the day turns out to be good but incredibly gruelling and we estimate that we must have walked close to 32 km with a climb of around 1,200 m. Rob takes us on the now mandatory short cut that nearly sends us plunging down a bank into a river, though we just manage to scrabble to safety. The map is sending him into mild but sustained apoplexy. I take a risk and suggest that he give up on the map and just follow the directions in the book and the route markers along the way, but somehow his orienteering spirit can't quite allow him to take this drastic step. His relationship with the map seems somewhat ambivalent; it can't fulfil his needs but he is still dependent on it, which of course puts him into permanent conflict. The therapist part of me wonders about the possible meanings that maps hold for Rob, perhaps about security or safety and the need for a reliable guide along life's rocky path. And then of course I wonder about my own struggle with maps, not only in the reading but also the fact that I feel very detached and disconnected from them, almost to the point of not caring. What does this say about my own internalised life map? I am happy to just follow the little red and white markers and trust that they will lead me the right way, whilst Rob distrusts them and has to re-assure himself that they are leading the right way. I guess for both if us, in our different ways, this journey symbolises something about our respective world-views. Still, I can understand his pleasure in knowing the lie of the land and the physical context of the landscape that we are part of and I wish I could overcome my petty resistance and join him in this pleasure.

Along the way, we encounter an odd bloke who we later imaginatively name 'Camping Guy 2'. He comes from Harrow, West London, has a big walrus-like moustache and walks with a very steady gait that gives the impression that he could carry on for days without stopping. We chat briefly, exchanging pleasantries, and then he ushers us on ahead. He is clearly a man who likes to walk alone, fortunately for us. Later on, while we are taking a break, he passes us again and I ask him if he is going all the way to Banyuls. He says, 'Yeah, unless I get pissed off with it and decide to go home.' This makes me laugh. Here we are, along with Craig and Lucy and the rest, nursing our injuries and thinking of justifiable ways out of this mad journey without losing face or seeming too pathetic, when we could just get 'pissed off and go home' – simple as that. In a sense I suppose we have become quite wedded to the path, the route and the idea of reaching our final destination of Banyuls. I feel quite removed from reality, indeed from humanity, and although the comings and goings of everyday life are never in fact that far away it also in some strange way feels a million miles away. So the idea of getting 'pissed off' and going home seems kind of incongruous and gives me a slight jolt of reality, which I guess is why it makes me laugh – as if I have recognised something about the context of this journey, or perhaps about myself. Still, one thing that I feel sure of is that whilst I have felt, and will no doubt continue to feel, pissed off at times, I don't intend to go home.

At the high point of the Col d'Anhaou (1,383 m) we see a sign that says 'SAINTE-ENGRÂCE 3H 30', so we know we still have a fair bit of walking ahead. The trail then drops downwards and takes us on the western side of the Gorges de Kakoueta and whilst the path hairpins steeply down through fields of grass and bracken, a series of barely noticeable signs indicate short cuts along the way, which we take with relish. Eventually we hit the bottom of the valley where we cross the river on a small concrete bridge and join a sizable main road.

The last few kilometres of the day involve a tedious and exhausting road walk into the face of the sun and for some reason we really push ourselves, striding at speed with the sweat pouring off us. As with most days, the last hour is always the worst as we begin to allow ourselves to think of an ice-cold drink and a good shower. We get a little bit lost, thanks again to Douggie's quaint but useless hand-drawn pictures of the village, but eventually, after ten hours of walking, find the gîte to a round of applause from Brigit and Craig and Lucy who are sitting outside the bar next door. Brigit looks like she has just been dropped off in a chauffeur-driven car. Craig and Lucy arrived about forty-five minutes ago, which means we have done really well considering the extra distance we have covered. All in all, we feel worthy, not only because we walked further than anyone else today but also because we chose to. We collapse into a chair and Rob knocks back three beers in as many minutes whilst I stick to juice and water in an attempt to re-hydrate. Together, we relish the day's achievement although we both feel drained by the effort. As we gradually recover talk turns to the fate of Corinne who has not been seen, but then after a while she turns up looking like she is about to collapse from exhaustion, barely able to speak. She has clearly had a tough day and seems to get lost quite a lot, having only what looks like a pretty basic guide to the route. She is a gentle and self-effacing woman with a good sense of humour and throws herself gallantly into the idle banter between us – and so it is good that the merry band of GR10ers are back together again. However, it turns out that this is Brigit's last day with us, as she was only doing a small section of the walk and tomorrow heads back to Toulouse. We agree to have a good send off for her tonight and Rob and I decide to push the boat out and go *demi-pension*, which means that we can thankfully forget about cooking and enjoy the local hospitality.

St Engrâce is a gem of a place, tiny but oozing charm and tranquillity. It seems to be just a handful of houses along with the 'Auberge Elichalt' attached to the gîte. The scene is dominated by a truly impressive eleventh-century church, and what with the view of the mountains rising up in the distance it is enough to just sit, drink and soak in the glorious atmosphere. We shower and claim a bit of bed-space on the very basic platform dormitory arrangement where we will be sleeping tonight and then have a look around the church, which is just as impressive from the inside with its Romanesque carvings and stone simplicity. The owner of the Auberge is Madame Burguburu, a forceful, no-nonsense woman who you would clearly want to remain on the right side of. After a beer in the bar we get the nod and all file upstairs to a large dining room where we are treated to a feast of soup, steak and rice that we agree is probably the best meal we have had en route so far. We toast Brigit with sincere fondness; this determined woman from Toulouse who led the way for us over the last few days. She speaks little English but that has somehow not been a barrier as we have just enough French between us to get along. She is remarkably stylish and well-groomed for a trekker, with her short blonde hair and expensive looking shades. She is quiet and self-contained, possibly due to the language issue, but I get the sense that she is comfortable in her own company. That said, she has been a good companion and we wonder who will take on the mantle of group leader now she will be leaving us. As we are considering this thorny question, Camping Guy 2 turns up and sits down at the end of the table, muttering to himself and fiddling with his moustache. Somehow, I don't think he is our man.

After dinner we go back down to the bar and sit outside for a final hot chocolate. Out of nowhere a truck pulls up and about ten tough-looking soldiers leap out and pile in for a drink. Meanwhile, Rob has fallen in love with the waitress, who we think is the daughter of our fearsome hostess. He says that she is his 'perfect woman' and I can almost feel him swooning as she passes close by. Quite what constitutes the perfect woman for Rob I'm not sure, but I think it is mostly the combination of dark eyes and a cheeky smile.

The night is long and hot. The platform bed is hard and uncomfortable and it feels like any available oxygen is being slowly drained from the room. I find myself between Rob and Corinne, the beauty and the beast so to speak, and it feels like around three in the morning before I finally fall into a fitful sleep.

DAY 12

ST ENGRÂCE TO ARETTE
LA PIERRE ST-MARTIN

After a good farewell breakfast for Brigit, we exchange emails and then off she goes, kicking up the dust behind her like the roadrunner cartoon. We have a climb of around 1,200 m today but a distance of only around 13 km, so it looks like it might not be too bad. Also, it seems like we are really heading up to the high country and entering another stage of the walk as we move further into the central area of the Pyrenees. We have enjoyed our stay in St Engrâce and Rob in particular has become quite fond of the place, although to be fair that might have something to do with Madame Burguburu's alluring daughter. Sadly, it's another case of unrequited love and Rob casts a few mournful looks behind him as we prepare to set off down the hill to the valley floor where the climb begins. But certainly, St Engrâce goes on the list of 'places we could live' and we think maybe we will return here one day.

The going is initially OK and we climb up steadily towards the head of the valley. The combination of the sultry heat with some pretty exotic-looking plant life gives the feeling that we are trekking through a kind of prehistoric landscape, something like Conan Doyle's *Lost World*. The heat is stifling and sweat pours off us as the climb becomes steeper. As we go I feel stronger and put on speed as I stride ever upwards. It really does start to feel that I might eventually be getting the 'mountain legs' that everyone told me about before we set off. But I am aware of Rob struggling a bit today in hitting his pace. We climb steadily up through the wooded side of the valley and then eventually break out into the open above the tree line, always a sign of the height that we have gained. We stagger on a bit further and then collapse in the grass for drink and a snack of apricots and chocolate. As we look behind us we are both stunned by the magnificent sight of the clouds below us, stretching out like a silvery velveteen carpet and broken only by the peaks of the mountains pushing through like little islands in this strange ocean sky. It seems amazing that we have walked through the clouds and now sit high above them looking down at a scene that I have only ever seen before from a plane. This is known as a cloud inversion, Rob informs me, and it truly is a breathtaking sight, not least due to the fact that we have got to this point through our own efforts. It is moments like this that the whole trip suddenly makes sense, as we breathe in the pure mountain air, relish in our physical exhaustion and sit atop the world in all its magnificent beauty.

We consult Douggie to check the route from here and see, to our horror, that he gives a warning about a particularly vicious sheepdog that guards the flock up here on top of the mountain. Apparently, many a walker has fallen foul of this dog and indeed it must have some considerable reputation to get a special mention from our trusty guide. I try to play down my growing anxiety whilst Rob seems totally unconcerned by this development and then, as we consider our options, we see in the distance a flock of a sheep and sitting upright in the middle of them all a monster of a dog. We are some distance away, but even from here the dog looks huge and seems to tower over the sheep that it's guarding. I say to Rob in my pretend casual voice that I have never seen a dog that's actually bigger than a sheep before and that maybe we need to take a somewhat more circuitous route than I think he has in mind, reminding him that he is my official canine guardian and it is important that he gives this role the full gravitas that it demands.

However, the Robster is unsettlingly calm and says that all we have to do is make sure we don't go charging through the flock and scare the sheep – as if that's what I am planning to do. We traverse the edge of the hill, keeping the sheep and the killer-hound a good distance away. I half expect that at any minute it will come bounding down the hill towards us and in my mind I rehearse the various defensive tactics that I might have to resort to, namely waving my stick around and hiding behind Rob. As it is, we make our way over the other side of the hill without incident. As we walk I spot a few men in the distance, hanging around a van and carrying what could be shotguns, although they could be sticks. I guess they are shepherds, of a sort, but I suddenly feel quite vulnerable and start to fantasise about being confronted by armed thugs who wait in hiding on the GR10 trail and pick us off as we go, a kind of Pyrenean version of *Deliverance*. I wonder how many times walkers have actually been attacked along the way and I also think about women like Corinne and Brigit, walking alone, and whether they ever feel threatened or vulnerable. I'm not sure I would want to do this walk on my own; the dogs alone would be bad enough, never mind the map-reading and navigating with a compass through thick fog.

During the morning's uphill walking I have become aware of some slight pains in my chest and I have to stop myself from slipping into worst-case scenarios in my head. I guess it could be muscular pain of some kind or maybe stress, although it's hard to believe I can really be experiencing a great deal of psychological stress during a trip like this. I recall a period some years ago when I had similar chest pains and after a trip to the doctor and a battery of tests it seemed that they were entirely stress related, but then that was a time when I was struggling through a very intense period of work. Whatever, having seen my father experience two heart attacks (and then drop dead from the third), the thought of congenital heart disease has never been that far away. Still, I put it to the back of my mind, denial being the best course of action at this point in time.

Over the course of the journey so far the two of us have been developing plans for our band 'Chough Eggs'. Why the name I hear you ask? Well, it's a long story, but suffice to say it involved a special Christmas day episode of the seminal ITV series *Doc Martin*, during which the post-food-and-alcohol-induced early evening slumber was abruptly broken when I jumped out of my chair and shouted 'chough eggs!' in sudden realisation of the gripping sub-plot that involved the illicit trade of rare bird's eggs in Cornwall. Fair to say, it isn't a real band as such. It's more of a virtual band, a kind of mutual fantasy that we both indulge in although we did actually have one get together many months ago when we played a few songs in my front room and even gave a somewhat informal performance at the annual BBQ of our infamously bad cricket team, The Swinging Googlies. Rob's got a great voice, folksy and pure, when he's brave enough to use it, and is also a fine guitar player. I play the piano, guitar and assorted bangy, squeaky things and as we have walked we have created an album in our heads with a pretty comprehensive track listing. As we reach the top of this particular climb and pass through an area with some farm buildings scattered around, Rob spots some small birds freewheeling around in the air with apparent delight.

With the help of Douggie's very useful nature section we identify the birds, to our joy, as choughs. As we watch them Rob says it seems like they are flying for fun and so there it is, the title of the Chough Eggs' first album: *Flying for Fun*.

We finally hit our high point for the day, the Col de la Pierre St-Martin, which sits at 1,760 m. The col is named after the boundary stone, the stone of St-Martin, which also marks the site of one of the better known annual Pyrenean rituals. Apparently, back in the fourteenth century something of a local spat developed between the inhabitants of the Barétous valley in France and the neighbouring Roncal valley in Spain. The dispute centred on grazing rights, no doubt the source of most disputes in times gone by, with the Barétous farmers sneaking their herds across the border into Spain to graze on the more lush meadow of the Roncal Valley. After many years of blowing each other's heads off with sawn-off shotguns (or whatever the fourteenth-century equivalent might be) a settlement was reached in 1375 in the form of the treaty of the 'Tribute of the Three Cows'. Word has it that this is the oldest treaty remaining in force in the whole of France and is still observed by a few thousand people every year on 13 July, when the villagers of Barétous hand over three symbolic heifers in return for the rights to use the pastures of the Roncal Valley. Apparently these days the three cows are given straight back again, but it's an excuse for a good knees up. Man, they know how to party in these parts. Unfortunately, we are a week early; it would have been great to have stumbled unexpectedly across this bizarre ritual along the way.

Eventually, we drop down into the ski resort of Arette la Pierre St-Martin. It's strange seeing a place like this in summer. Without the snow it looks ugly and somewhat depressing. The ski slopes are great tracts of brown earth and scree cut like scars into the hills. It looks like a great hand has come down and raked its long nails across the mountainside. The cable cars hang lifelessly and the seasonal holiday accommodation consists of some pretty grim-looking concrete blocks, like seventies Haringey. If anything, the place reminds me of a ghostly *Scooby Doo* fairground. Still, I bet it looks great in the winter; it's amazing what a bit of snow can do. We manage to finally get to our destination, the Refuge Jeandel, which is run by a very eccentric bloke who is hobbling around on a broken leg. He is something of a joker, cracking one-liners with gusto and not put off by the fact that we don't understand a word of what he is saying and just look at him with puzzled expressions on our faces. The refuge is relaxed and easy and already fairly full with a collection of pretty chilled-out-looking walkers.

Craig and Lucy are there to greet us, having pipped us by about an hour. They are clearly making a claim for Brigit's pace-setting title. I have become quite fond of Craig and Lucy. Craig has a great sense of humour and is clearly something of a prankster. Lucy is also good fun, and together they make a great couple. We have a few beers together and discover that there is a house guitar, which we proceed to play around on. The owner gets very excited and says we must play to everyone during dinner but we fend off his advances with our feigned ignorance. I say to Rob that this could be the first gig for Chough Eggs but the idea of playing in front of real people makes him anxious and I am not sure I can quite pluck up the courage myself.

There is no sign of Corinne and we wonder whether she has got lost, which she seems to do on most days. Corinne has a novel approach to walking the GR10. She just sets off in one direction and keeps going, oblivious to any markers or signs; and I thought I was bad. We worry a little about her and I think of those dodgy men I saw lurking around on the hillside with their shotguns. We have a little free time and so take a wander around the 'ghost resort'. Douggie mentions that there is a launderette, though it is with more hope than optimism that we bag up our dirty clothes and bring them along. But amazingly, there it is. A launderette and a good-sized shop, which means we can wash our clothes and stock up on much needed provisions. This really is a bonus day. I volunteer to do the clothes and it feels great to be sitting in a warm launderette waiting for the cycles to complete. I have always liked sitting in launderettes, for some strange reason. I'd ask my therapist about that, if I had one.

I ring Nicky and Jess and have a good long chat with them both and Jess plays the piano down the phone. They seem to be having a nightmare with some old friends who have descended upon them, mid divorce, and poor Nicky has had to deal with World War Three breaking out and screaming kids (and grown-ups) all over the place. Talking to her does compound a sense of guilt about being away and the fact that I am not around to support her with this.

While I wait for the laundry, I see Corinne pass by and give her a shout. We have a brief chat in which she tells me that she did get lost and followed the GR10 signs in the wrong direction and ended up doing an enormous loop to get back on track. Another Corinne GR10 variation. She has planned ahead and booked one of the empty holiday apartments, clearly in need of a bit of comfort and mod cons. I guess she is a Parisienne.

Back at the ranch, everyone is getting ready for their three-course meal whilst we maintain our solid trekking credentials by insisting on cooking our own. Well, Rob does. To be honest I would have gladly sat down and got stuck in with the rest of them but Rob, in the true spirit of camping and economy, asks our joker of a host if there is anywhere we can cook. With a look of mock disdain on his face he gestures outside to a tiny shed in at the end of the garden, and after a bit of exploration and rummaging around amongst old chairs and badminton rackets we find a gas cylinder and small one-ring burner. Rob is in his element though, enjoying nothing more than a good culinary challenge, and to his credit knocks up a superb dinner of pasta and chorizo topped with melted cheese. Even Craig says that our meal was much better than the one they had and I have to begrudgingly admit that there is something special about cooking and eating your own food after a long day's walking. Rob is generally right about these things. Overall, we have a pleasant evening, sitting outside drinking beer and chatting. Out of nowhere, the garden suddenly fills up with a herd of huge horses and it feels slightly surreal, sitting there amongst these snorting, farting beasts (although to be fair it reminds me of any night in a bunkhouse). Rob's roving eye has fallen upon an attractive woman who seems to be walking with a friend. The verdict of myself, Craig and Lucy is that they are a gay couple, but Rob will have none of it and christens her his 'Dark-Eyed Girl'.

DAY 13

REFUGE JEANDEL TO LESCUN

I wake up feeling crap. The room was hot and stuffy and I think I must have lain awake for hours. Still, we get breakfast down us and prepare for another day. It looks like we have about 15 km to cover today, most of it being downhill, which is a change. Once again we are the last to leave, Craig and Lucy having set off about an hour before us, and these late departures are getting me down. I guess time has always been an issue for me. I generally arrive early for everything in my day-to-day life and have little time or toleration for tardiness. But then this adventure is all about compromise, one way or another, and I mustn't get too anal about these things. It's funny; people tend to view me as pretty calm and laidback: in reality I am generally quite anxious, but just good at covering it up. Rob is pretty slow in the mornings, or maybe I'm too eager. I'm sure there are enough things about me that are probably driving him mad, like my refusal to engage in any form of map reading or my general sense of vague indecisiveness. Finally we head out into a heavy mist that is rolling up from the clouds below. Due to a combination of the lack of visibility, Douggie's poor directions and the 'fucking useless' maps, we can't find our way out of the resort and spend about half an hour wandering about in vague circles. Rob's fixation on how bad the maps are somehow makes him study them even harder, perhaps in the hope that they might magically transform themselves from 1:50 to 1:25 through the sheer power of thought alone. I tentatively suggest we just forget the maps and follow the directions in the book, but this doesn't go down too well. After some time and more than a little frustration we eventually find our way onto the footpath and get going on our way.

The first stage of the day's walk takes us through a very spectacular limestone landscape, sculpted and twisted through thousands of years of erosion, and it reminds me of a seventies location set from *Dr Who* or perhaps *Star Trek*. The going is pretty difficult, as we have to pick our way through the stony ground, but the views are stunning as the clouds roll around below us. As we walk, occasional ripples of thunder echo across the valley, a reminder of some distant storm far below. Through the cracks and fissures of the limestone push a veritable feast of colourful mountain flowers: violet campanulas, dark blue irises, alpine clover and delicate pale yellow buttercups. Rob particularly loves these flowers and takes great delight in spotting new ones along the way. My knees feel good and for the first time since leaving St-Jean-Pied-de-Port I have not taken any Nurofen.

Still, for some reason I feel pretty crap today, on the emotional front. I feel tired generally but also just low and homesick and I have to contend with the urge to throw in the towel and call it a day. I fantasise about getting a train home and surprising Jess and Nicky as I roll up unannounced at the door, although at the same time the idea of quitting is simply out of the question. If this really was an episode of *Star Trek* I could just beam myself home for a few hours but, as it is, foot power is all we have. About an hour or so into the walk we come across Rob's Dark-Eyed Girl and her friend standing consulting their map. They must have been going very slowly for us to catch up and they do seem pretty relaxed about the whole thing. We offer a fairly weak 'hello', not knowing what nationality they are, and then leave them behind with a wistful look from Rob. I tell him again that popular opinion amongst the GR10 community is that these two are as gay as gay can be but Rob isn't having any of it.

After a further half an hour or so of picking our way across this limestone plateau the path suddenly veers sharply upwards and cuts across the top of the ridge at the Pas de l'Osque at 1,922 m. The last few metres up to this crossing point is quite a scramble that involves us having to slip off our rucksacks and haul and squeeze ourselves through a gap in the rock, passing our rucksacks to each other as we do so. It almost feels like rock climbing and is an exciting variation from the usual walking. From here the stony path leads more or less downhill for the rest of the day with stunning views of the high Pyrenees all around us.

We come across a large group of elderly day-walkers picnicking in a field and it is comforting to know that we are close enough to civilisation for a bunch of oldies to make it out here for a day trip. I have been looking forward to reaching Lescun as, according to Douggie, it is one of the most attractive villages along the route – already I have put it on the 'places to live' list. Part of me has been seeing this trip as a genuine opportunity to check out that fantasy house in the Pyrenees, the one I have always dreamed of, and in my dream world Lescun may be just the very place. The weather is sunny and pretty warm today, although that changes as we begin to make our descent through the cloud that's been lying below us. Now and again we hit a 'poncho moment' and both transform ourselves into our temporary versions of Quasimodo to prevent the heavy, water-laden air from breaching our clothes and rucksacks.

Soon, we come to a break in the cloud cover and we catch our first glimpse of Lescun, far in the distance. My initial reaction is to feel a little disappointed, not helped by Rob remarking that the place reminds him of a 'north Wales council estate' – all grey slate and bleakness. Already I find myself defending Lescun, this place that I have idealised in my mind. As we reach the outskirts of the village we are amazed to see Corinne a hundred metres or so ahead of us. Somehow she didn't get lost and has hit a fairly steady pace of her own. We hail her down and walk into town together to find the gîte, the Refuge du Pic d'Anie.

It's a comfortable place and so far we are the only people staying. Corinne bags a little room all to herself, leaving Rob and me to fight over the thirty or so remaining beds. We each choose a bed about as far away as is possible from each other, I guess seeing this as respite from the nights of enforced intimacy over the last couple of weeks. Later on another guy arrives and strangely chooses a bed right next to me, so I move my stuff to another bed across the room.

That night we eat in the only place open in Lescun, a good traditional bar/restaurant, and have a great communal three-course meal that consists of soup, chicken with couscous and pureed apple for dessert, all washed down with a carafe or two of the local red wine. Craig and Lucy are here, having of course booked themselves in to the only hotel in town, as are an assortment of new GR10ers, and we all gather together around a number of tables quickly knocked up by the owners of the bar. It makes me think that these places, in the middle of nowhere and on the route of the GR10, must be perpetually invaded by backpackers and trekkers, probably bringing in much-needed custom. A mad, wild-eyed French guy comes into the restaurant and sits down next to me at the table. We recognise him from last night at the Jeandel, where for some reason I can't quite recall, Rob christened him 'Erection Man'. As I accommodate his rather expansive settling-in routine next to me, I remember that last night this guy had shared a small dorm with Craig and Lucy, and slept in the bunk above Lucy spooking her out a bit with his general oddness and lack of clothes. As we were preparing for bed, Rob in his wisdom spooked Lucy out even further by painting scenarios for her in which our friend lay all night in his bunk above her, in some deranged psychotic state, toying with his unfeasibly large penis whilst fantasising about her downstairs. Rob has that special charm when chatting to women.

Anyway, I attempt to make a little casual conversation with Erection Man but he just glowers at me fiercely so I back off and leave him in peace, the miserable git. Craig entertains us by informing us that the sole of his boot has come off and so is now tied to his boot with a piece of string. We applaud his optimism and guile but can't help but question whether this arrangement will get him through the next 480 km. After the meal, Rob and I sit up at the bar for a last red wine and apparently, as we hear relayed to us later on, Erection Man makes some caustic comment about typical *Anglais*. Well, screw him and his giant penis, that's what I say.

DAY 14

LESCUN TO BORCE

We rise at 7 a.m., good for us, and make our bleary way over to the hotel where, for some unknown reason, they provide the breakfasts for the walkers in the refuge. Rob is muttering about his Dark-Eyed Girl and bemoans his bad luck that she must have stayed in the one other gîte in town. It was, apparently, a fifty–fifty situation that could, if it had fallen the right way, have changed the course of his life forever. I just yawn and scan the breakfast table for coffee. We are the only people in the room. Elvis Presley is playing at a surprisingly robust volume for this early time of day and an odd woman with an Elvis hairdo and a bit too much bling for someone of her years arrives to serve us breakfast. She clearly has something of a fixation with the late Mr Presley, although the only memorabilia on show is that of the hunting kind: large stuffed heads of deer and wild boar. She should really have Elvis' stuffed head up on the wall, but that might not go down too well. A basket of toast is produced and each time we finish it she magically produces another. This happens several times and we begin to wonder about sitting in this strange room all day, eating toast and listening to Elvis. For about two seconds we consider the possibility with some seriousness, the sheer folly of the idea appealing to us both, but then haul back our sanity from the brink and stumble out into the street.

Craig and Lucy haven't left yet and we spend an hour or so with them and Corinne, generally faffing about as we prepare to leave. I do a bit of unpacking and repacking of my rucksack, ever hopeful that it might suddenly become a couple of kilograms lighter, and Craig straps his flapping sole back onto his boot with his handy piece of string. Another couple are with us, elderly and Dutch, who have impressed us with the fact that they undertook the last two stages of the walk in one go. The notion of 'doing a double' is something we have considered but not yet managed, and it is an act of GR10 bravado that is held in high esteem. Funnily enough, last night we met another Dutch woman walking the GR10 in the other direction. She said it was because she preferred the sun on her back. Most people, like us, walk the GR10 from west to east because the mornings more often than not involve a steep climb and if you leave early enough you can complete most of it in the shade. To be honest though, this didn't really occur to us and the main reason we are walking east to west is because the guide books told us to. Also, and here's the best reason, I would much rather plunge into the warm Mediterranean than the Atlantic after a walking a gruelling 850 km.

There's a nice old village feel to Lescun, with narrow twisty alleyways and lovely old stone buildings with red-tiled roofs. Though we only have time for a little look around, I do like the place, and it feels much better on the inside than seen from the outside. I can see how it has acquired a reputation as something of quintessential village, although Douggie may have over-egged it a little. Rob is not so impressed and strikes it off his list of places to live. It's fair to say though that our personal criteria on this front are quite different. I like quiet places in the middle of nowhere where I can live out my hermit fantasy. The fewer people the better; perhaps one bar. Rob is after somewhere a little livelier and with a bit more action going on, a bit of hustle and bustle perhaps.

Anyway, it looks like a pretty gentle stretch today, around five or six hours with a climb of only 600 m. Now, when we consult Douggie over breakfast each morning, anything less than 1,000 m looks good to us and is even greeted with cries of 'yeah, easy', 'no worries' or 'piece of cake'. It's funny how one's judgements change over time. As mentioned, my only training for this trek was a stride up Box Hill in Surrey, which apparently stands at 172 m high, and this has now become my preferred unit of measurement as we approach the big climb of the day. So it's not quite four Box Hills today, which feels highly manageable and it's with a little spring in our step that we head out of Lescun with Craig and Lucy, Corinne and our unnamed 'Double Dutchers'.

The walk up and out of the valley from Lescun is beautiful; lush, green, laced with sturdy looking farmhouses and the whole area looks incredibly fertile. We pass houses selling cheese and honey; chickens running around in fields; and the whole ambience is one of the purest serenity. We push on at a good pace, leaving the others behind and it seems, unbelievably, that we have cemented the role of group pace setters after the departure of Brigit. As it turns out, the climb, although less than previous ones, feels really difficult and seems to go on forever as we push initially through the bracken-skirted path and then up through the wooded side of the valley with Lescun disappearing out of view. The GR10 signs are easy to follow, although not to be confused with the numerous red and white markers daubed on the tress by the local foresters. Why they choose to use such a similar mark is beyond us, or maybe it's simple mischief on their part. The path zigzags its way up the steep, forested hill and eventually, after a long and sweaty few hours, we get to the day's high point, the Col de Barrancq, which sits at 1,601 m. It's a superb spot and we crash out for some lunch under a tree. We also leave three sweets on top of the marker post for Craig, Lucy and Corinne, little nuggets of encouragement from today's group leaders.

For the first time on our journey there are times when I find the walking a little tedious. Not exhausting, painful, relentless or any of those kind of things, but just tedious – and I wonder if I am beginning to get bored with the experience. Every day, up to the head of a valley, over the top and then down to the bottom again: it does feel a trudge sometimes. Still, the tedium has been relieved slightly by Rob, who has been working his way through a complete performance of *Chitty Chitty Bang Bang*, rounded off with a particularly fine rendition of 'Posh'. Rob is a musical waiting to happen – he just can't resist a good song and the chance of a bit of dressing up. No doubt Julie Andrews will put in an appearance at some point soon. He also does a very annoying version of 'Chu-Chi Face' that involves him grabbing my cheek and giving a firm tweak between thumb and forefinger. Of course, he knows it annoys me so he just can't resist doing it, again and again, which amuses him no end. Oh well.

We take the path downhill, gently looping through open fields, bracken and eventually woods until we hit tarmac and make our grateful way into Borce, which sits across the river from Etsaut. The two villages lie close enough to almost be one but they are completely distinct from one another; Etsaut being a pretty functional place whilst Borce is beautifully historic and well-preserved and clearly something of a tourist attraction; hence the locals mostly live across the river in Etsaut. I immediately like Borce, and attempt to persuade Rob that we should have a rest day tomorrow so that we can sit and soak up its tranquil atmosphere. In most of these places along the way the mountains loom up around us, but this village really sits in the base of a tight valley with walls of rock rising up on both sides and the road and river snaking their way along the valley floor. Rob is not convinced and the debate continues as we stroll into the village and find our way to the really very pleasant *gîte d'étape*, which has a relaxed feel and a great kitchen for a spot of home cooking.

It seems we are the first of our group to arrive and so we maintain our status as leaders and are quite chuffed about the decent pace we are managing. As we settle in the Dutch couple arrive and then later a guy who looks just like Harold Shipman, the notorious GP serial killer. I remember seeing him a few days ago and it turns out he is also going all the way to Banyuls, one of the hard core. He seems to be a nice guy, although I can't help but wonder whether he will creep into our dorm in the middle of the night and pick us off one by one with his opiate syringe. The Dark-Eyed Girl is also in residence and Rob attempts to pluck up the courage to go and talk to her.

'You know she's gay,' I say, but to no avail as in his mind she is The One. Of course Rob doesn't get around to talking to her and so we get no further in this particular debate.

Whilst I knock up a tuna risotto Rob goes down to check out the bar, which apparently has an Internet connection, so that he can look up the chords for 'Posh' and work them out on the ukulele. I chat to Corinne for a bit, sitting around the table with a few of our fellow walkers. It's the first time I have really spoken to her properly and I like her gentle calmness and ever-present smile. She continues to remind me a little of Audrey Hepburn, in nun-mode, and I have this fantasy of her as some kind of lapsed Catholic and perhaps someone who is burdened by a lot more than the rucksack she carries on her back. This notion is reinforced when she tells me that she once walked the Camino de Santiago, the Way of the Pilgrim, and the therapist part of me is intrigued by her motivation for this present quest. She talks about the stresses and strains of modern life and the need to find a sense of inner calm amongst the madness of the modern world. And she is curious about Rob and me and our own personal motivations for undertaking this journey. I talk a little about the idea of the mid-life crisis and the extent to which this might have been something of a personal motivation for this adventure. On reflection I wonder about this. The notion of a mid-life crisis seems such an indulgent and somewhat middle-class and peculiarly male construction; the domain of the 'worried well' perhaps. Hardly a crisis, but there is I think a point, a mid-way point in life, where one glances both behind and ahead and reflects upon what has been and what is to come. A sense of 'taking stock' I suppose, and in many ways that is what this journey is about; a brief punctuation in life's complex narrative. Corinne is reassuring and supportive and her words always delivered with smile.

After we eat we go for a wander around the village and cross the river to check out Etsaut as well. The two villages of Borce and Etsaut are split dramatically by a newish-looking highway that passes through a tunnel under the Col de Somport into Spain. Also running through the centre of the two villages are the rusting remains of the old railway line that used to go from Pau to Zaragoza, again through the huge Somport tunnel. Apparently in 1939, towards the end of the Spanish Civil War, hundreds of fleeing republicans used this line to be transported though the Pyrenees, to be later placed in refugee camps at Gers, near the town of Oloron-Sainte-Marie. As we walk, small swift-like birds swoop down, darting around inches from the ground like the fighter ships from *Star Wars* as they attack the Death Star. Rob is especially taken with them, calling them the 'Stunt Birds of Borce'; and they are really quite something to watch. Later, I manage to impress Rob with a little limerick that I make up while we are ambling around:

> *There was an old man from Borce,*
> *Who farted with incredible force,*
> *He exclaimed 'Zut Alors!'*
> *And then farted some more,*
> *And felt much better, of course.*

OK, so it's not Edward Lear but not bad for the time of day. The effort of walking around is too much for me and we stagger to the bar for a red-wine nightcap. It has a shop round the back and we buy a few things for our lunch tomorrow. The owner of the bar is a formidable woman called Eliane, of mature years but with enough energy to power a small town – but then I guess that's what she does, being the owner of the only bar. Eliane jokes and teases us, whilst topping up our glasses with merry abandon, and we like her immensely. We christen her the 'Force of Borce' and we soon ascertain that the permanently exhausted looking young guy also working in the bar is her husband. He must be about twenty years younger than Eliane but if she is as energetic in the bedroom department as she is in all others then little wonder he looks so knackered. As we sit sipping our wine I pluck up courage and tell Rob about the pains I have been getting in my chest over the last few days. He takes the news with remarkable calmness, considering my repressed anxiety, and we agree to sleep on it and see how we go in the morning.

I lie awake for what seems like hours, my mind drifting with the ebb and flow of the sleeping breaths all around me. My brain goes into overdrive at these times, perhaps compensating for the lack of external stimulation. It's as if I've just had a double espresso, thoughts racing and going off on tangents galore. I know I just have to wait and eventually sleep will come.

DAY 15

BORCE TO GABAS

This morning we tackle the Chemin de la Mâture, a dramatic and somewhat vertiginous 1.2-m wide and over 1-km long path cut into the cliff side 150 m above what in Spanish is known as the '*Las Gorgas del Infierno*' – Hell's Gorge. It's going to be a long, steep climb. Once again we are the last to leave the gîte, having just waved off Corinne who is almost as slow as us in the morning. Being not too good with heights, she's anxious about the cliff path and we agree that if she gets worried she will wait for someone to accompany her, either us or someone else along the way. I wonder whether the GR10 was a great choice of walks for someone not too keen on heights. Anyway, we head out of Borce and up the side of the valley and soon begin to traverse the Chemin de la Mâture, the Path of Pines. As the valley floor drops away beneath us we are struck both by the spectacular nature of the path and the physical feat of its construction. The roughly hewn path was hacked out by prisoners in the eighteenth century in order to fell the tall pines growing on the mountainside. The trees were then floated down-river to the coast where they were made into masts for the French fleet. Scorched holes in the rock face suggest that it might have been blasted with dynamite and we wonder how many lives must have been lost along the way. If this were England, railings would line the edge of the path and health and safety notices would be plastered all over the place like some kind of corporate graffiti. But here there is just the edge of the path and a sheer drop of several hundred feet. It's at times like this that I become acutely aware of the weight of my rucksack, the way it sways and lurches with any missed step, and I think it wouldn't take much more than a bad stumble to send some poor hiker toppling into oblivion.

After about an hour of walking, when we are perhaps halfway along the path, I again begin to be troubled by the nagging pains in my chest. What worries me most is that I only seem to be getting the pains when I exert myself and I keep having visions of the small sign on the treadmill in the gym back home that says something about seeking medical advice if you experience dizziness or chest pains while exercising. I fall behind a bit while Rob strides on and I feel myself plunging into a state of anxious despair. I can't help but think about my father who booked his final passage to the underworld after suffering his third heart attack, and whilst the whole experience of this walk has in many ways brought me closer to the spirit of my father, himself a great walker in times gone by, I had not really intended to follow quite so closely in his footsteps.

My mother sometimes used to refer to my father as the 'Wandering Jew' and indeed he was something of a nomad, his professional life as a well-respected orthopaedic surgeon taking him all over the world. He was at times a restless soul, that's for sure, as he sought to escape Churchill's 'black dog', and the process of walking helped I think to channel some of this restive energy. As a child, I often recall him returning from one of his walking trips and presenting me with an interesting stone or two from his travels. I also remember the post-Sunday-lunch outings when he used to round us children up for a short walk 'around the block' that was in fact much more like 8 km, which is a marathon for a small child. I must have been six or seven years old, buzzing around him like a miniature satellite, always careful not to venture too far out of his paternal orbit; he would be walking slowly, surely, reassuringly along the country lanes that eventually led the way through the patchwork of fields and back to our Sussex home. One field usually had corn in it and I was small enough to run ahead, sneak into it and jump out when he got close. It never frightened him of course. The other field was a meadow, stretching down towards the lake in the far distance. Interesting, the paths that we follow through life. But as I say, I am not quite ready to follow my father down life's final Grande Randonnée.

I also think about Nicky and Jess and begin to fantasise about what would happen to them if I dropped dead here upon the wayside. I find myself trying to visualise Jess' face, thinking I may never see her again, and then I struggle even to picture her face in my mind. Jesus, am I forgetting what my own daughter looks like? Now the anxiety and despair is compounded by guilt; the daughter whom I abandoned, who was left bereft through my own reckless folly. I wonder if Rob knows how to deal with a potential heart attack. Most likely not and there's probably no mobile signal around here. As my mind whirls I fall further behind and stop to rest more frequently to allow the pains to subside.

Rob has picked up that all is not well and comes back down the path to check out how I am doing. Unlike other days when I have experienced the pains and said nothing, I decide it is time to come clean, so I pluck up the courage and let him know that I am feeling pretty worried. All credit to Rob, without batting an eyelid he says we should head back to Borce where we can stay another night at the gîte in the hope that I can see a doctor at some point today. He jokes about the lengths I am prepared to go to get an extra rest day and says that he doesn't want me dying 'on his watch'. I am also acutely aware of how magnanimous this is of Rob, as to turn back now means that he may lose the trail of the Dark-Eyed Girl that he has been obsessing about for so long now. But still, turn back we do and begin to make our sorry way back down the path. I feel thoroughly miserable and a little ashamed, and, unseen by Rob, a few tears roll down my cheek. I think to myself that this could be the end of the walk and that no doctor is going to allow someone experiencing chest pains to continue such a journey. I imagine the humiliation of returning back home with 'failure' stamped across my forehead in large letters.

After an hour or so we arrive back at Borce and whilst Rob returns to the gîte I go to the bar to ask Eliane about a doctor. With hardly a pause for thought, she rings her own doctor who has a practice in the next village about 12 km away and tells me that he can see me at 12 p.m. – in about half an hour. Blimey, I think. If only getting a GP appointment was this simple back home. Eliane has already achieved near mythical status in our eyes and now I start to believe that she could transform the NHS if somehow we could smuggle her back to England and unleash her powers in the right direction. However, such is 'the Force of Borce' that, like a genie out of a bottle, it would be impossible to predict what could happen in such circumstances. I have hardly even begun to think about the logistics of getting to see this doctor in half an hour when Eliane introduces me to Philippe, who is at the bar having a coffee. Philippe is a kindly young guy who it transpires makes a living delivering wine to the local bars and cafes in the area. He happens to be heading off to the doctor's village right now and, downing his espresso, gestures for me to accompany him to his van, pronto. As we walk out of the bar I bump into Rob's Dark-Eyed Girl and her friend, just preparing to set off for the day's trek and amidst all the anxiety and uncertainty I find time to marvel over the fact that here is a couple who set out even later than we do. Anyway, with no time even to let Rob know what is going on I find myself sitting in a van and being driven off to god-knows-where. Philippe turns out to be an expansive chap, full of good humour, and as we head off down the road he tells me that he plays bass guitar in a Rolling Stones tribute band. I guess this makes him Bill Wyman. He says that he has a gig on Saturday night but goes on to explain that he never earns any money playing music, hence his day job of delivering wine. As a musician myself I come to the conclusion that some things are simply the same the world over.

Philippe asks me why I am going to see the doctor and in my pigeon French I try to explain about the pains in my chest and walking the GR10. *'Ah, le cardiac!'* Philippe bellows with great gusto and laughs uproariously. I am not sure whether to be alarmed or reassured by this response, but somehow I feel comforted by simply being in his presence and the seductive movement of the vehicle zipping along the road, this of course being the first time I have been in a car for a couple of weeks. I tell Philippe again about the GR10 and my plan to walk all the way to the Mediterranean, and that I hope to resume my journey tomorrow after seeing the doctor. Philippe lets out another tremendous guffaw of laughter and says, 'Ah *oui*... perhaps in a box.' He laughs so much I worry he might drive us off the road, but, somehow, I can't help but join in and together we chuckle about the image of my coffin being passed along the GR10 via the hands of a long line of backpackers.

As we enter the village Philippe points out the bar where he is playing on Saturday; he's clearly more concerned with his impending gig than he is about me dying of a heart attack. In our brief twenty minutes together I feel quite fond of Philippe, with his hearty laughter at my misfortune but kind and unaffected action. As he drops me off outside the doctor's we shake hands and I wish him well with his gig on Saturday night. Likewise, he wishes me well with the walk and then clutches his chest dramatically with barely concealed mirth. God, these French.

I make my way up the path to the surgery, let myself in and sit in a waiting room with a mother and her young son. I feel a little incongruous in my shorts and walking boots. Will this be the end of my little adventure as I am sent packing back to Blighty? I wonder if Rob will carry on the walk on his own and sincerely hope that he will. We had briefly discussed what would happen if one of us dropped out, for reasons physical or psychological, and both tentatively agreed that the show must go on. The mother and son are soon called in and quickly ushered out and then the doctor himself appears at his door and beckons me to enter. He is a big, genial looking man and strikes a startling resemblance to a middle-period Michael Gambon. We shake hands and he gestures for me to sit down at his desk as he himself sinks into a luxurious-looking leather chair and assesses me with curious contemplation. I notice the half-finished packet of cigarettes lying amongst the piles of papers on his desk.

'*Bonjour, monsieur…?*' he says smiling, leaving me a healthy pause to jump into.

'*Err… Le Vay. Monsieur Le Vay,*' I say. He raises an eyebrow, nods knowingly and slips effortlessly into English, albeit with a beguiling and strong southern French accent. For some strange and irrational reason I begin to think of him as my father.

'So what seems to be the problem Mr Le Vay?', Dr Gambon gently enquires, although I have the feeling he has been well briefed by Eliane. Actually, I think many of the more distinguished men of the locality have been well briefed by Eliane over the years, so to speak. I go into a hesitant and faltering explanation of my predicament and he asks a few questions in a very nonplussed, casual manner. How frequent are the pains? How long do they last? How heavy is my rucksack? He stands up, walks around the desk and asks me to stand up and then proceeds to poke and prod my chest and, interestingly, finds a spot right between my ribs that is really quite sore when he exerts a sharp pressure with his fingertips. After this somewhat cursory examination he walks back to his seat and relaxes back into his comfy chair. I half expect him to put his feet up on his desk, light a fag and pour himself a large brandy.

'Well, Mr Le Vay,' he announces with a faint smile and twinkle in his eye, 'you may continue your journey to Banyuls-Sur-Mer.' I don't know whether to laugh or cry. Instead I just sit there like a lemon, albeit a lemon in shorts and walking boots. Dr Gambon goes on to explain that he does not think there is a problem with my heart and that the pains are being caused by the weight of my rucksack. I make a mental note to tell Rob that I need to lighten my load but stop short at asking the Doc for a note. 'It's your bones,' he says, and mimes the action of the rucksack pulling my rib cage back and creating pressure around the sternum. That's it, consultation over. He pulls out some paperwork, charges me €25 and goes into a lengthy explanation about how I can claim the money back on my insurance when I get back to England. Somehow, I don't think I'll bother.

Emerging from the doctor's, I feel light-headed with relief and optimism, a feeling only slightly dulled by the fact that I now need to make my way back to Borce. It seems that hitching a lift is my only option and so I amble out of town, find a good spot and stick out my thumb. Oddly, the idea of walking the 12 km back to Borce only briefly crosses my mind and is quickly dispensed with. I realise haven't hitchhiked for about twenty years and it actually feels quite good, a kind of return to the days of my youth. After about ten minutes a kindly woman picks me up and takes me half way, followed by a silent and wrinkled old farmer in his battered Citroen who goes out of his way to drop me off in the centre of the village.

I find Rob sitting outside Eliane's bar drinking coffee and fill him in on my little French medical adventure. He's relieved to hear that I'm OK and then starts up again about the girl 'with the beautiful eyes' who left this morning and somehow I know that he is forever going to blame me for this failed romance. Dream on, monsieur. Anyway, we celebrate my return from the near-dead with a game of table tennis on the table that sits invitingly in the village square outside Eliane's bar. I beat Rob two games to one and as we have a drink to cool down Eliane challenges me to a game later on. A knowing chuckle ripples around the smattering of locals hunched against the bar drinking wine. With seemingly little choice I accept the challenge and we agree to rendezvous for the big match in the bar at 8 p.m.

We amble back to the gîte to mooch around and cook ourselves some dinner and Rob in fact knocks up a very fine cassoulet created from a giant tin of *confit du canard* (preserved duck) that we bought across the road in Etsaut. As usual he makes enough to feed the entire gîte (and some of the village) and so, as our fellow walkers sit down to their meagre portions of dried soup, chorizo and three day old bread, we tuck into a feast of gargantuan and faintly embarrassing proportions. It feels odd, because having missed a day we are out of synch with our travelling band of GR10ers and from late afternoon a new wave of walkers begin to waft in on the Pyrenean breeze. This includes, funnily enough, another Scottish couple that provide an instant replacement for Craig and Lucy, Harold Shipman of course and a tall and willowy mysterious young lad who we come to know simply as Shepherd Boy. He actually is in fact a young shepherd, from Switzerland, who is apparently walking the GR10 as a way of finding out about how the Pyrenean shepherds manage their flocks; a kind of fact-finding sheep research project one could say. Maybe he's doing a BA. He's only seventeen, travels with just a sleeping bag and umbrella, sleeps in churches along the route and cadges food as he goes. He speaks no English but with a little translation we learn that for this night only he has splashed out on a night in a gîte because he is being slowly driven mad by the incessant chiming of church bells inches from his head. It's a tragic irony that of all the gîtes along the 850 km of footpath our poor friend has ended up in one that is slap bang next to the village church – even Douggie warns his readers that if they want a peaceful night this is the one place not to be. We offer Shepherd Boy some of our cassoulet and he wolfs down the lot with undisguised glee. We like him instantly and only wish we could talk with him more freely.

As we sit digesting our food in peaceful contemplation there is a commotion at the door and our hearts sink, just a little, as Camping Guy 2 blusters in, bristling moustache to the fore. We thought that with his clockwork pace he would be a day or two ahead of us, but he tells a sorry story about being bitten by a dog and having to find a doctor for a rabies jab. I wonder if he saw my friend Dr Gambon but keep quiet about my own little sorry adventure, like some kind of shameful secret.

It's just before 8 p.m. and, feeling too full for comfort, I have to prepare for the big game. Rob jumps around and waves a towel around in my face and I take a few deep, sharp breaths to calm the nerves. The folks in the gîte wish me luck and as we open the door and stride out into the square the bells chime the hour with a keen intent. It might be 8 p.m. but it feels more like high noon as we saunter down the steps to the bar. Eliane sees us come in, grabs the bats and launches herself over the counter like an *Exocet*. She must be nearly sixty but her energy and enthusiasm for life is exhausting to witness. The bloody bells go off again and the few bar proppers give me encouraging looks.

As we take our positions at the table I ponder my strategy. I don't want to embarrass Eliane as she has clearly been looking forward to the game, but also don't want to be condescending and let her win. I guess we will probably play a couple of games, maybe best of three, so I reckon we can win one game each and take the last game to the wire and she will leave with her dignity intact. 'Just one game' she says, and we play a few warm up rallies. She's pretty good for an old girl.

We launch into the first game, which quickly becomes fast and furious. Eliane plays a blinder and beats me 21–15. '*Encore*,' she says and this time beats me 21–18. 'And another,' she shouts and plays like a whirling French dervish. Sweat pours off me as I put all I have into just keeping her at bay. I am on the back foot all the time and apart from a few attacking shots feel that I am simply holding back the inevitable.

Between points I glance around to see that a few of the locals have gathered to watch, as well as the folks from the gîte and Shepherd Boy who is hugely entertained by the whole spectacle. Amongst it all, I notice a young boy, perhaps eight or nine, sitting on a wall and watching intently. Eliane continues to attack relentlessly and it is like playing some kind of superwoman.

Whilst I put up a gallant fight I get totally whacked five games to nil. I'm a wreck; Eliane looks pristine. We shake hands and she takes us back to the bar for free drinks. Like some kind of proud Amazonian warrior she announces to her audience that this sorry English loser has just had his arse whipped by a grandmother. She gestures to the boy, who was sitting on the wall and who I realise now is her grandson. Total, utter, but somehow very pleasurable, humiliation.

Later in the evening we lose the water supply to the gîte and then Eliane bounds in to tell us that the whole village has had its water supply cut off, something to do with a broken pipe. Thankfully, the village 'fountain' still provides a constant supply of fresh spring water from the mountains and Eliane brings buckets of water up to the gîte and stations them in the toilets for our use. If ever such things as genies existed then Eliane would be my one of choice.

DAY 16

BORCE TO GABAS (AGAIN)

I have a bad case of déja vu as I wake up and contemplate the day ahead. Hmm, the Chemin de la Mâture, I know that one – didn't we do it yesterday? We have breakfast and do several trips to the fountain to get water and make sure we leave some full buckets of water stationed around the gîte. I have enjoyed our stay, apart from the small matter of the cardiac drama, and it is with some sadness that we go down to the bar to bid farewell to Eliane, the Force of Borce. She really is something, probably the best character we have met along the way, and we pledge that we will go back to visit some day. Rob and I hatch a plan to set up a table tennis academy down the road in Lescun so that Eliane is confronted with a steady stream of shit-hot ping-pong-playing trekkers. That'll teach her.

All tooled-up with food and water, we prepare for what feels like a new stage of the walk as we head up into the highlands of the central Pyrenees. We have a long 25-km walk ahead and a 1,500-m climb to the high point, the Col d'Ayous, so we know it's going to be one hell of a long, tough day. Still, that's only about nine Box Hills, which makes it sounds a little more manageable.

I still feel worried about the chest pains and doubt the doctor's opinion, pessimist that I am, but I try to put that to the back of my mind and as we stride out of the village we immediately bump into Craig and Lucy. They apparently took a day off so that they could go into town somewhere and buy new walking boots for Craig. Somehow it seems we are destined to do the whole walk with our Scottish friends. I feel a little sad that due to our enforced rest day we are out of synch with Corinne and may not see her again for the remainder of the walk. I'll miss her serene smile and wise words.

Once again we make our way up out of the village and along the narrow path for the Chemin de la Mâture, and Rob makes several remarks about how the scenery looks strangely familiar. Anyway, we soon get beyond the point that we did yesterday and I pretend that I am feeling ill and need to turn back. Rob, with the merest of pauses, says he knows a good doctor in the village down the road who looks a little like Michael Gambon.

As we continue we really start to gain some height and the views are spectacular – snowy mountain peaks stretching all around us. After an hour or so we reach the Cabane de la Baigt de Sencours (1,560 m), a small and very basic walkers' cabin that at a push could sleep five or six people on a raised sleeping platform. From here we head south, traversing the valley side and eventually arrive at the bottom of a cirque that sits below the Pic d'Ayous. A cirque ('circus' in French) or corrie is a concave, amphitheatre-shaped bowl that sits at the head of the valley and is formed by the process of glacial erosion. The 'bowl' has been scooped out of the mountain side by the glacial ice and its abrasive passenger rock and forms something of a cup with a lip on its lower edge. Seasonal melt-waters will often form a tarn or corrie lake, a great favourite of Rob's who likes a spot of wild swimming given half the chance.

From here the path winds its steep way up the west side of the bowl and we finally reach the high point of the Col d'Ayous (2,185 m) and stop to eat lunch with Craig and Lucy by the edge of the lake that sits invitingly below the Pic du Midi d'Ossau, the blue-grey summit that dominates the landscape. It's cold this high up and we put our fleeces on as we sit eating bread, cheese, chorizo and chocolate while Craig kindly knocks us up a cup of tea with his handy little gas stove. There are a lot of people around and we realise that this is quite a popular spot for day-trippers. Down in a bowl by the lake is the Refuge d'Ayous, an impressive-looking place that immediately makes us want to stay there, although we can't really justify stopping so soon after losing a day. Rob reckons his Dark-Eyed Girl might be staying there tonight, and he is probably right seeing that they left Borce so late yesterday. Rob mentions her probably about once every twenty minutes now, so I just nod and glaze over. He makes me promise that when we get back to England I will track her down using all my powers of detection and somehow bring them together in a whirlwind of romance. No problem, I say. Leave it to me.

It's a long, steep descent down into Gabas, ending in the obligatory road walk and bad attack of pancake foot all round. Eventually, at some point in the early evening, we get to the Refuge de Gabas, a rather dingy gîte with crap showers and cramped accommodation, although we do have a good meal. Funnily enough, Camping Guy 2 and Erection Man are both in residence and in reasonably good form. It turns out that Camping Guy 2 is in fact Steve from Harrow, which brings us crashing down to reality with a bang. I had forgotten that Harrow even existed. I can hardly work out what day it is anymore and it can take Rob and myself an hour or two to work out what the actual date is; that is if we can be even bothered to try. I am not sure if, during the course of this walk, I am becoming stupider or whether my brain is just naturally pruning off all the useless knowledge and information that is simply surplus to requirements. Let's face it, the most we have to think about is putting one foot in front of the other and following red and white markers (or a map, in Rob's case).

We indulge in a smattering of conversation with each other and our fellow walkers, but that is really just about it. Sleep, walk, eat, sleep, walk, eat – and so on. I am finding it harder to visualise people and faces back home and the idea of my job as a child-therapist is becoming increasingly abstract. It is like there is a whole part of me that I am slowly losing touch with. I only hope that there is a new part of me that I am starting to connect with; otherwise the outlook is not great. I'll arrive in Banyuls a dribbling, wide-eyed, catatonic wreck, which probably isn't quite the reunion that Nicky and Jess had in mind.

Another odd thing is that when Rob is walking ahead of me he occasionally morphs into other friends, almost as if he becomes some kind of composite of other people I know. I really don't know why this is; perhaps it's a compensation for some kind of sensory deprivation or a projective thing in the sense that Rob becomes a blank screen for my mind to play with. So, not only am I losing touch with who I am but I am also losing touch with who Rob is.

I start to think how strange it would be if we both actually physically changed as we walked along, regressing into more primitive versions of ourselves with protruding foreheads and jutting chins, grunting and scraping our knuckles along the ground and chasing bears with sticks. I think actually I am rather tired and need to go to sleep.

The dorm is terrible; we are crammed in like proverbial sardines and I feel that I might suffocate from lack of oxygen. The beds are so short our feet hang over the bottom. As the cacophony of snoring, wheezing, farting and coughing starts up around me I lay awake, staring into the black middle-distance and wonder if I have truly entered hell. 'Abandon all hope, ye who enter here' I believe was the inscription on Dante's ninth and final circle of hell. Yes, well – I am on the verge of abandoning hope in this trekkers' inferno. The odd thing with my insomnia is that I can be on the verge of total exhaustion, my body craving the chance to rest, but as soon as my head hits the pillow it's like a little light bulb pops on in my head and my mind goes into overdrive, just at the point when I am on my own, in the dark, trapped, with no-one to talk to and nowhere to go.

My insomnia survival kit of torch and journal doesn't really help much and I feel self-conscious about doing too much hamstering about in case I disturb anyone. The earplugs are great but I do worry that I might push them in too hard and get them stuck in my ears. I don't think I could cope with another trip to the doctor. When I was a child, I think around seven or eight, I pushed the dwindling remains of a rubber into my ear during a PE lesson at school and it got stuck there for about two years. I always knew it was there but was too embarrassed to say what had happened, and after a while I just kind of accommodated myself to the fact that I had a rubber in my ear; my own special little eraser-shaped secret. Anyway, eventually I went to the doctor for some kind of check up and he syringed my ears and lo and behold out popped the little rubber onto his metal dish. He said it was a bit of chalk and I told my mother that it must have fallen into my ear one time when I was lying on the beach at Seaford in Sussex, during a family trip to the seaside.

Funnily enough, a number of years ago I was lying in bed and a little spider crawled into my ear. For several days I could feel this funny tickling sensation and I kind of knew that the spider was in there but managed to conjure up sufficient denial to prevent myself from thinking about it too much, which of course comes from living with a rubber in my ear for two years when I was a young child. Anyway, about two weeks later I was attending a group training event for social workers and I felt a tickling sensation, gave my ear a flick and the spider flew out, landed on the floor and proceeded to scamper out into the middle of the group as if to make some kind of important contribution to the process. I wonder if it complained to its spider friends about being stuck inside a human.

DAY 17

GABAS TO GOURETTE – THE CENTRAL PYRENEES

After a predictably awful night comes a terrible morning: with a group of walkers getting up at about 6 a.m. and continually slamming the door to the dormitory. It's like being woken up by a large hammer repeatedly thudding into my skull. Rob is really pissed off with them. At breakfast, the obligatory bread and jam, we saw our friend Shepherd Boy stroll in, cadge some food and disappear again and we wonder which old church he was sleeping in last night.

We slowly get ourselves together and are ready to leave at about 8 a.m. The process of rubbing Vaseline into our feet and toes continues to be a very fixed morning ritual and in a way serves as both physical and mental preparation for the day's walking. Also, I have not suffered a single blister so far, which seems quite amazing given the distance we have walked. We've got a nine-hour, 22-km section today with a 1,400-m climb and it's going to be another long old day on the road.

Although neither of us likes the mornings, we don't feel too bad and I think it is with a little relief that we get back into motion again. Walking has become a form of meditation in many ways as mind and body become attuned to each other, and the gently rhythmic and repetitive motion seems to focus the mind and allow the trials of last night's dormitory hell to wash away. In fact, I can understand how 'walking meditation' is a method of mindfulness practised by many Buddhists. The route takes us down the road for about ten minutes and then we cross over into some beech woods and start climbing up the side of the valley. After half an hour or so of undulating walking we come to the Corniche Alhas, which consists of a twenty-minute stretch along a very narrow path with a pretty much vertical drop inches to our side. There is a helpful sign that reads 'Passage Vertiginous', which gives a little clue to the potentially hazardous nature of the route, although this time the French have excelled themselves with a handrail that the health and safety brigade would be proud of. With a sheer drop on one side for 500 m, we are both actually very grateful for the presence of the handrail.

Shortly after navigating the Corniche we come across Shepherd Boy who is sitting eating an apple and waiting for his sleeping bag to dry, which he has spread out in the morning sun. He must have had a wet night and we stop and exchange a few broken phrases and words, his English being negligible. We press on and get to the point, which we get to every day, when according to Douggie the 'serious climbing begins'. Why does he have to say that? Every damned time? Anyway, he's right and the going gets really tough as the path zigzags its way steeply up through the forest and we move down a gear into 'little step mode' as the gradient becomes too great for proper walking. We dovetail with Shepherd Boy, exchanging chocolate and apricots as we pass each other, and eventually the landscape begins to open out as we climb beyond the tree line and emerge into a wonderful open vista, the path traversing high up on the side of the valley, with the wonderful sweep of the valley floor opening up below us. Far across, on the other side of the valley, we can just pick out Le Petit Train d'Artouste, a little tourist train that takes people up to the Pic de la Sagette at 2,031 m. It looks fun; just a shame that it's on the wrong side of the valley.

Suddenly, it is turning into a truly spectacular day. The views are stunning, the sun is warm on our faces and it feels like the best walking of the whole trip so far. I feel overcome with contentment and the affirming sensation that this is what the whole thing has been about, this very moment right now. The countryside is beautiful and Rob especially continues to be bowled over with the vast array of beautiful wild flowers that line our way. They are gorgeous little designs of creation and he takes great delight in noting the new ones; and indeed it is interesting to chart the regional changes in our environment as we make our slow way along this great mountain range.

Rob has also been checking out the changes in architecture along the way and noted a distinct difference as we moved out of the Basque region into the more central High Pyrenees. The changes in style and structure of the buildings, the shape of the roofs and colour of the tiles have all been noted and there really is something quite unique about travelling at a pace where the smallest changes in our surrounding can be observed in this manner.

After a couple more hours of pretty steep ascent we see a motionless figure in the distance and as we get closer we see that it is Corinne, leaning against an old stone wall. We are pleased to see her but she looks exhausted, drained of energy and possibly tearful and it becomes apparent that she is struggling and having some kind of existential crisis, wondering whether she should turn back or try and carry on and get to Gourette. The effort of the walking is clearly taking its toll and she says she is close to quitting completely and heading back to Paris. We chat for a bit and gently encourage her to carry on and at least get to Gourette and see how she feels then. We are pretty much halfway on today's section and it seems crazy for her to turn back now.

Corinne also tells us that someone up the line has been robbed of their stuff while they were taking a rest and upon further questioning it turns out to be Erection Man. We half-heartedly suppress a chuckle at his misfortune and are grateful for this little bit of GR10 gossip. After a while we leave Corinne to reach her decision and hope she chooses to continue. I like her and she lifts my spirits with her friendly smile; it would be sad to see her throw in the towel.

Further on we catch up with Craig and Lucy who have crashed out by a stream that's bubbling its watery way down the mountainside. The two of them are upbeat and cheerful, as they always seem to be, but they say that they are also finding the walking incredibly exhausting and much more difficult than they anticipated. Interestingly, they are both qualified scuba divers and they tell us about some of their diving trips, looking at old ship wrecks and such like. They embarked on this trip as they had some time on their hands and wanted to do something completely different, but they are clearly re-evaluating the experience and talk longingly about diving expeditions in the warm waters of the Red Sea. We join them for lunch and take turns at dunking our heads in the stream. The pure cold water is unbelievably refreshing and several times I fill my hat up and slap it on my head with glee.

The final section of the climb is becoming really intense and it takes all our effort to push on, step by step, up to the peak of Hourquette d'Arre, which sits at 2,465 m. The view is staggering and we stand stupefied through a combination of exhaustion and the stunning panorama. The vast range of snow-topped mountains seems to envelop us and it hits us that we truly have entered the central High Pyrenees. Large areas of snow still remain and we jump around in it and throw snowballs at each other. Looking back we see Corinne, a little ant in the distance, slowly making her way up the slope and we are pleased that she has chosen to continue.

While Craig and Lucy head on down towards Gourette we decide to wait for Corinne as she is clearly struggling. Just as she is about to make the last few metres to the top, gasping for breath and her face pale with exhaustion, Rob jumps out and announces that the GR10 is closed for repairs and that she will have to turn back. Corinne collapses and mutters something about the 'zilly engleesh zense erv umairr', but I think she is glad that she pushed on and made it to the top.

The descent is a real killer and I still find it so much harder going downhill than up, as my knees protest sharply at the pounding they are getting. As it is starting to get quite late and a mist is coming in quickly, it strikes me how easily one could become lost up here at over 2,000 m. In fact, we do get a little lost for about twenty minutes but soon get back on track and continue downwards. We stop now and again to wait for Corinne, or at least make sure that she can see where we are, partly to give her encouragement but also because her track record is not so good on the getting lost front and at this late stage of the day we want to make sure she is OK. Ironically, it's Rob and I who get it wrong for the last part of the descent and we end up having to edge our way down a ski slope, which would be fine with skis and a bit of snow, but on foot it's an exhausting and tedious process and is a real killer on the legs. Of course, poor Corinne follows us thinking we know what we are doing and also ends up having to pick her way down the slope.

Finally we get to Gourette, a rather depressing ski resort, and after walking for a solid eleven hours I am feeling sick and dizzy and close to the point of collapse. We find the gîte where Craig and Lucy are already tucking into their evening meal and as I am on washing duty I use every last vestige of energy to shower, wash out our pants and socks and then collapse into a chair to eat. Afterwards, we all go out for a drink together and I start to feel vaguely normal again. Corinne seems to have decided to continue for the moment, which we are all glad about, although for how long I am not quite sure. We have a small room to ourselves, which is a welcome relief after last night's torture, and so I lie down and slip into a blissful coma.

I have been having some pretty weird dreams over the last few nights, remnants of which I remember for a short while before they are burned away by the heat of the morning sun. Sex, burning heads, death, all manner of emergencies and frightening wild dogs have all featured strongly and I wonder what my poor unconscious is up to. Too be fair, my dreams (when I do manage to sleep) have always been pretty much on the strange side and many a time Nicky has been awoken by my dreamtime exertions, so to speak. Still, I wonder what the unconscious impact is of walking in these vast open spaces, the mountains ever-present and the separation from all that's familiar. Does the landscape of my inner psyche become equally shaped by this dramatic Pyrenean panorama? Or does the open space and absence of the usual level of inter-personal stimulation allow it to become populated with the fears and fantasies that are normally kept at bay by my mind's defences?

DAY 18

GOURETTE TO
ARRENS-MARSOUS

Today it's a gentle five-hour stretch with a measly climb of 600 m; after the last two days it comes as one hell of a relief. It's a strange turn of events when five hours of walking feels like a day off.

The five of us walk pretty much together for most of the day, the stony path taking us through a forest of beech trees and then up and out into more open landscape of fields and pasture. At one point Craig and Lucy go off ahead for a period and end up going the wrong way and have to climb an extra few hundred metres to get to Col des Tortes, the high point of the day. As a result of their navigational mishap we get to the top first with Corinne and are busy tucking into lunch when they come staggering into view. The sight of Craig's red face accompanied by much cursing and bluster causes us all to laugh furiously. He's is not amused, but after catching their breath they join us for lunch.

It's a pleasant and gentle stroll down towards Arrens-Marsous, through green fields of horses and cattle. Suddenly Craig lets out a massive yell and tears off down the hill, taking quick, snatched glances behind him as if being chased by a bull or some other crazed animal. Of course, we see him go and instinctively hare off after him only to see him moments later creasing up with laughter. He's well and truly got his own back for our laughter earlier.

As we walk into town we can't resist a bar with tables nestling in the shade of the plane trees and sit down for a pre-gîte beer. Arrens-Marsous is a small, peaceful place and has a smart, well maintained quality about it with its white-walled, grey-roofed buildings and well-tended open spaces. There are two gîtes in the town, one that only does *demi-pension* and another that has a kitchen for self-catering. Rob is keen that we cook for ourselves, although I would rather stay with the others who are doing the *demi-pension*. I like the sense of being in the group and the general feeling of camaraderie, and this could possibly be the last night we are together.

Lucy's Achilles is really playing up, to the point where she can hardly walk anymore and she is going to have to rest for a couple of days if she wants to continue. This seems to have got worse quite quickly and I feel sorry for her, having had to struggle with my own painful knees earlier in the walk. I appreciate that Rob is concerned about our budget; I think also he might be getting a little tired of our companions and might want us to break out on our own, which I can understand. But after discussing it he magnanimously agrees to do the group thing.

The Gîte Camelat happens to be a pleasant place; clean, comfortable, attractive and well looked after, and at a cost of €30 for a bed and evening meal it seems a pretty good deal. In fact, the food is superb and we tuck into *confit de canard*, potatoes and salad washed down with a carafe or two of some very mellow red wine.

It turns out that it is Bastille Day today and a French national holiday. The little town of Arrens-Marsous is celebrating with a firework display so we all decide to go out for a drink and then head down to the sports ground on the edge of the town where it's taking place. Rob is having a bit of a wobble tonight, a minor emotional collapse seemingly brought on by a desperate need for a cigarette. Over the last couple of weeks he has smoked very little, tending to buy some fags and then throw them away again. Anyway, it turns out that the possibility of buying cigarettes in Arrens-Marsous after the shops have closed is zilch. We scour the few bars and hotels with no luck and of course the more we try the more desperate Rob gets, to the point where we start to harass people around us, but somehow tonight it seems that the entire population of the town have gone smoke free. Craig teases him mercilessly – to the extent that Rob has started calling him Lex Luther, the arch villain from *Superman*. Rob does seem seriously tired and a little stressed out and says he doesn't feel up to walking tomorrow, and I wonder if he is hitting the proverbial GR10 wall.

Down at the sports ground we stand around for ages waiting for the fireworks, but when they do arrive they are pretty spectacular. The French are good at these things, but then they have enough *fête* days to get the practice in. Most of the townsfolk seem to have turned out and the air is alive with the crackle, bang and fizz of the fireworks and the smell of the deliciously aromatic sulphurous smoke that's being whisked around on the late evening breeze. There is much laughter and the excited chatter of little children; and of course the mandatory 'oohs' and 'ahhs' of an appreciative crowd. After the show we amble back to the gîte and it is 11.30 p.m. by the time we hit the sack, but feels like 3 a.m.

DAY 19

ARRENS-MARSOUS
TO CAUTERETS

Today we have a twelve-hour 27-km stretch to Cauterets looming ahead and it is with a sense of deep foreboding that we sit down to breakfast. Douggie recommends that it is best done in two stages; stopping after about six hours at the refuge D'Ilheou at the peak of the climb. Craig and Lucy's guidebook says it can be done in a day but it would be one hell of a walk. Lucy has been advised by the local doctor to rest up for a day or two, so the two of them have booked into the gîte for a second night. Corinne sets off and plans to do the six hours up to the gîte at the top. The weather is blistering hot; Rob is still ambivalent about whether he wants to walk today and I can feel myself wavering. It's amazing how easily one's will can begin to crumble. So far, the two of us have supported each other, pulling each other through our respective moments of weaknesses and lapses in motivation, but today we are both borderline and Rob's wavering is infectious. All in all we both feel totally exhausted and I guess we are feeling the cumulative impact of almost three weeks continuous exertion as the daily grind really begins to take its toll.

DAY 19

Having said that, there is another side to our mutual wobble. Today is Saturday (we think) and we happen to know that tonight some great Bastille Day weekend celebrations are being planned in Cauterets, and we both agree it would be great to be there for the party. We could possibly do it in one stretch but we would be physical and emotional wrecks by the time we got there and fit only to collapse, so the thought of getting to Cauterets by means other than walking is very tempting. We finish breakfast and half-heartedly get prepared to leave, deciding only at this point that we will stock up for lunch at the patisserie across the square and then decide what to do from there, although I think we can both feel that we are slipping inexorably towards Plan B, which involves walking up the road and sticking out our thumbs.

We prevaricate a bit more, lingering outside the patisserie as if about to embark on some kind of pastry-based crime. The idea of skipping a day's stage is a struggle to contemplate. Have we got all this way only to cheat ourselves at the first sign of weakness? Isn't this truly the time to dig in and show our mettle? Will we look back at this moment with regret for the rest of our lives as we recount our adventures to our grandchildren over tea and scones in front of a blazing winter fire?

On the other hand, though, what's the big deal? We have walked about 400 km and climbed the equivalent of Snowdon most days over the last three weeks, so is it really that terrible to take a day off and skip a few kilometres – which is really all we are talking about here? God, the power of rationalisation; I would make a terrible addict. But still, we do note that Douggie makes several references to people hitching short sections of the route now and again, the tedious road sections, and also taking the odd short cut, so we don't think we are entirely flying in the face of GR10 protocol by skipping a stage.

As we loiter suspiciously outside the patisserie we get distracted by the attractive young woman through the window dishing out the croissants and baguettes and our conversation turns to the question of how all patisseries in France are staffed by good-looking women, whereas most bakers back home are normally staffed by the baking branch of the Addams Family. We come to the conclusion that French women are generally more attractive than their English counterparts (although this is partly due to the alluring accent) and so, on a percentage basis, one is more likely to find more attractive women working in a patisserie than in a bakery: so it is probably not the case that patisseries have a a higher percentage of good-looking women working in them compared to other similar French food-based outlets.

Blimey, forget rationalisation, what about the power of procrastination; are we going to stand here all day discussing the aesthetic merits of the French patisserie trade? We go in, confront the object of our desires, resist the temptation to undertake a quick questionnaire on her employment history, bag a baguette and a couple of croissants and head down the road to find a good place to hitch.

I can't believe how good it feels to stand at the side of a road and stick our thumbs out. I haven't hitchhiked for about twenty years, apart from my recent adventure with the doctor in Borce, and the change in our routine – not to mention the thought that we have not got ten hours of walking ahead of us – induces slight hysteria. We make bets about what colour car is going to stop and very soon a car does stop and we throw ourselves in, hauling our rucksacks in behind us. It's a friendly young chap who takes us a few kilometres up the road, where he drops us off and heads up towards a paragliding centre where he is working. He tells us we should have a go some time. A little later, a very kindly woman stops for us and drops us at the nearest town from where we catch

DAY 19

a bus to Cauterets. The whole experience is very surreal. The simple experience of being in a car and in a bus and the motion of travelling by vehicle once again seems incredibly strange. We are getting somewhere without moving our legs!

We disembark at Cauterets station, a strange and totally incongruent building that has been made to look like something out of the Wild West, giving the sense of being on a film set. But as we walk through the town we immediately like the place. There is a lively, buzzy feel about it, enhanced by the fact that they are clearly gearing up for the Bastille Day festivities. Bands and buskers roam the streets, the cafes are brimming and after our virtual isolation from the rest of humanity the place is a feast of noise and colour.

There are huge signs and banners all over the place proclaiming 'Latin Roc' and it seems as if this is the theme for the festival, which sounds good to us. Of course, this is the largest place we have been in since St-Jean-Pied-de-Port, which feels like months ago although it is only a couple of weeks or so, we think. We have a little wander around, feeling slightly culture-shocked and still a little phased by the manner of our arrival, and take stock with a drink in a cafe in the main square.

After that we pop into the *office de tourisme* where, inevitably, Rob falls for the girl working behind the desk and coaxes her into telling him in her broken English about the schedule for the day's celebrations. She seems very young and I warn Rob that his intentions, although possibly honourable, may not be entirely wise.

With the help of Douggie we hunt out somewhere to stay and at the second attempt find a gîte that has a great self-contained flat around the back that we can have to ourselves. It's like our own little place and so we move in and just chill out for a couple of hours, revelling in the sense of comfort and freedom. Tomorrow is declared a rest day (our second official rest day) and we plan to hit the town tonight with a vengeance.

After getting the practicalities out of the way, the launderette, the shopping and a fair bit of sitting around playing ukulele and harmonica, we head out to find something to eat and get tempted into a restaurant that has a guy outside cooking up a great dish that looks like a cross between paella and fish stew. We discover that it is a traditional tomato-based Catalan dish called zarzuela, very rich and full of interesting seafood, and so we find ourselves a table, order a carafe of local red wine and tuck in. As we eat and drink we stray a little from the mundane and talk about more personal matters, reflecting upon our respective childhoods and the struggles therein. Somehow, the two of us, tucked away in a bar in this town, deep in the folds of this ancient mountain range, feel a little like lost souls. I wonder what it is we are each looking for within this journey; what it is that drives us each day, step by step, towards our goal.

Anyway, the zarzuela and red wine have done the trick and we stumble back out onto the streets of Cauterets. The place is still buzzing with Bastille Day fervour and we eventually find ourselves down by the Wild West station where, to our amazement, several thousand people have gathered for a huge outdoor concert. We catch a bit of the last band and then suddenly, provoked by a blast from the booming PA system, everyone breaks into an extended bout of ceroc dancing, a kind of Latin salsa thing that I only know about because it became quite popular back home for a while. It's amazing to watch these young people dance the night away with such style and cultural verve. If this were England, it would just be a mass of drink, vomit and the occasional fight.

So in a diplomatic attempt to address any Anglo–Franco dance-related issues, and fuelled by plastic tumblers of lager from a large temporary bar that has been erected alongside the square, the two of us lurch around in a very non-ceroc kind of way, our movements somewhat dictated by our aching bodies. Rob has a kind of funky hand thing going on that is very impressive and I dance in the only way I know how, which according to Jess is something akin to an old bloke looking for something he has dropped on the floor. Still, who cares? We party with abandon and for possibly the one and only time in my life I manage to drink Rob under the proverbial table.

As the evening draws to a close we are treated to an impressive firework display accompanied by classical music and some commentary about French independence. It's all quite moving really, in a bleary-eyed kind of way, and at 3 a.m. we weave our way back through the crowds and collapse in drunken exhaustion.

DAY 20

CAUTERETS – REST DAY

After our Bastille Day session it was about all I could do to collapse into a semi-comatose state. However, the benefits of sleeping through the night are trashed by the fact that I feel like shit. My head pounds, my body aches, my throat suffers the foolish torment of too many cigarettes and the only slight relief from this predicament lies in the knowledge that I don't have to walk anywhere today. God that feels good. In fact, it far outweighs my shittiness and suddenly I feel OK, if just a little rough.

It feels great to have a flat and some space to ourselves after so many nights of dormitory hell. Between us we cook up a gargantuan breakfast (good forward planning from Rob on the shopping front yesterday) and just enjoy hanging out in our special pad, feeling pleasantly full and drinking coffee. The gîte is a family-run business and as we sit outside blinking in the late morning sun the women of the family bustle about cleaning, doing the laundry and watering the plants. They joke and chat as they work and occasionally respond to our attempts at communication, and the overall feel of the place is pleasantly maternal. It feels a little like we are part of a French film, some unknown story being played out around us and the rich ambience of the environment wraps around us like a warm haze. We could live here we think, or perhaps just hang out for a few days in this little bubble of perfection. The bells of the cathedral begin to chime in the warm breeze and the mountains rise up above us on all sides. Cauterets, like many of these Pyrenean towns, sits in a valley and is firmly wedged in by the surrounding rock. Cable cars run up to the top with a whir and a buzz but all is mostly quiet after the night's festivities.

I speak to Nicky and Jess on the phone; as ever it is lovely to talk to them and I get sharp pangs of homesickness. Nicky sounds stressed as she has to cope with the emotional process of scattering her father's ashes, who died just a couple of months ago, whilst managing the highly draining family friends who are still visiting and continuing with their messy marital separation. The timing of this trip wasn't great, especially in the context of the loss of Nicky's father, and we had spoken about postponing it for a later time. But Nicky, to her credit, felt that I should do it: that life must carry on, one way or another. Still, I feel guilt and a little shame at not being there to support her; leaving her while I indulge in this petty folly of an expedition.

I suddenly feel very low, my bubble burst by this sharp needle of reality. Jess has things going on at school and again I feel I should be there, the guilt of an absent father. It makes me think about my own father, absent for long periods of my childhood, both physically and psychologically. I have strived so hard since Jess' birth to be a different kind of father, but does this make me just the same? No: I don't think so, but that knowledge doesn't make me feel any better.

We go for a wander around town and get some of the practicalities done, like laundry and shopping. Cauterets is a thermal spa town, as are many of these places along the way,

and parts of it are very Victorian, a little like Tunbridge Wells
but without the 'disgusted'. We come across the old bathhouse,
a grand sulphurous affair with *'Les Sources'* carved in stone
above the entrance. Rob likes this and declares this his stage-
name for our band, Chough Eggs. I tell him it sounds like the
name of some dodgy old northern comedian, which appeals to
him even more.

DAY 21

CAUTERETS TO LUZ-ST-SAUVEUR

We're up early this morning and a breakfast of poached eggs goes down well. We've got something like a seven- or eight-hour walk today and a climb of nearly 1,000 m, which is somewhere in-between OK and bad. Last night our little band of GR10ers was once again reunited, but today we head off first leaving Craig and Lucy to follow. Corinne is left behind as she has decided to take a rest in Cauterets and then maybe do a shorter route tomorrow. We will be well and truly out of synch by then so it looks like this is farewell. I'll miss having Corinne around. She's been good company and her calm, benign influence has been good for all our spirits, I think.

The trail meanders gently up through a pine forest and we get glimpses of Cauterets behind us, nestling below in the folds of the valley. Rob has grown very attached to the place and it has become number one on his 'Places I Would Like To Live' list. As we walk we hatch a scheme for Rob to buy up an old building and turn it into the coolest *gîte d'étape* on the GR10. It would be a funky gîte, we decide, with good jazzy, funky music being piped into the dorms, comfy furniture and perhaps some tasteful North African furnishings. Rob would do the cooking, knocking out lashings of chorizo stew and fine red wine.

It's quite hard to get going again after the rest day; although physically I don't feel too bad, it's more about the psychological motivation to continue, which kind of drifts off if we stop for too long in one place. Still, we trudge on as the path gets steeper until we finally emerge from the forest into an area of open grassy slopes that lead the way up to the Col de Riou, which sits at 1,949 m. The views from here are good, although the scene is somewhat marred by the trappings of the winter ski season.

We drop down for a long descent into Luz, the path hair-pinning its way down through the steep wooded slopes and once again the last hour is a real killer of a road walk, the hard surface playing havoc with our feet. I think my feet are actually changing shape. I looked at them the other night in the shower, and thought they looked like the feet of a hobbit, kind of flattened out and squashed. Will I have deformed feet by the end of the trip, I wonder?

All in all, it has felt like a pretty tedious walk today, of the kind that the GR10 throws up every now again. Nothing special, nothing spectacular, just a routine stretch that has got to be done. Luz is also nothing special, or maybe that's because we are not in a particularly receptive mood: I don't want to be unfair to the little place. Like Cauterets, it's another spa town and probably had its heyday towards the end of the nineteenth century when the combination of sulphurous waters and mountain air was a big attraction.

We book ourselves into an OK gîte and shower in a tardis-like contraption in the corner of the bathroom. Later we have a walk around town and find a spot for an evening picnic, which actually involves eating the lunch that we didn't eat earlier. Rob buys himself a traditional French beret that suits him well and eventually we meet up with Craig and Lucy again for a drink and few games of cards. They got lost again today, which amuses us no end. It isn't long before we crash out, knackered and feeling a little drained in spirit.

DAY 22

LUZ TO BARÈGES

Bread and jam gîte breakfast is pushing Rob to the brink of insanity. One of these mornings he is going to flip and there will be a major Anglo–French *petit déjeuner* diplomatic incident. Someone will end up with egg on their face, or jam in this case. Actually, I don't mind the bread and jam and I quite like the hard cold toast thing the French do. But Rob just pushes it away with disdain and reaches for the coffee. He tells me that when he opens his funky gîte in Cauterets he will serve splendid breakfasts of eggs, bacon, mushrooms and Toulouse sausages, followed by lashings of Frosties, Weetabix and coffee. His breakfast would be the talk of the GR10 community and Douggie would be compelled to give the gîte a five-star rating, based purely on the breakfast.

After 'breakfast' we Vaseline ourselves up, pack our rucksacks and set off at the respectable time of 8.15 a.m. – pretty good for us. I also slept reasonably well, only slightly disturbed by Rob's thrashing about in the night. I don't know if it was a bear or a *sanglier* that he was doing battle with this time, but it sure was a hell of a fight. He was probably wrestling with a fearsome slice of bread and jam the size of the Eiffel Tower.

DAY 22

Thankfully, we have only a shortish five-hour walk today and a moderate climb of around 600 m. However, the ascent is steep and the sun hot and soon both of us are puffing and sweating away like anything. Some of these stages are deceptive, lulling you into a false sense of ease before hitting you with a killer gradient. When it is as steep as this we slow our pace and just take little steps, conserving our energy as we wearily make our way up to the head of the valley. It's a good stage though, once the climbing is done, and the gradual descent into the next valley is truly beautiful as we walk through fields laced with wild flowers and butterflies galore, spinning around our heads like living confetti. Only the nasty biting flies disturb our contentment.

We stop for lunch by the stream that runs through the floor of the valley: bread and pâté followed by a large orange each. We are going through an orange phase at the moment and it has to be said that they are incredibly tasty and energising after a few hours on the trail. The walking though feels easy now and there is a spring in our step as we set off again, sauntering pleasantly along and gradually beginning to drop down towards Barèges.

I have had a few twinges of the chest pain I experienced earlier but feel reassured by my visit to Dr Gambon that this is muscular rather than anything more sinister. My knees feel OK and altogether I am feeling reasonably fit. I feel less obsessed by the weight of my rucksack, unlike earlier in the walk: if anything it has become more of an extension of myself and I have become adept at adjusting the various straps as we walk to give the pressure points around my shoulders and hips a bit of respite as we move along. There's no grim road walk this time into town, just a gorgeous stroll through colourful woodland; this probably goes down as one of our more pleasant re-entries back into civilisation.

Barèges is another sizable place, a ski resort in winter and also another thermal town, so 'Les Sources', the legendary

Chough Eggs' frontman can rise again. Rob makes the point by occasionally slipping into character, although I think he sounds a little more like Les Dawson. There are a couple of gîte options available and after finding no-one at home at our first port of call we try the L'Hospitalet, a rather enormous and daunting place that apparently used to be an old military hospital. We book ourselves in and actually end up with a great little room to ourselves, which is always a happy relief from dormitory hell.

We have a wander around and what with the range of odd characters shuffling around, trekkers and walkers nursing their various ailments and other people who just seem to be hanging around, the place feels a little like an asylum. I half expect a fat nurse to come along, pin us to the floor and inject us up the arse with Largactil or some other kind of anti-psychotic drug (I've seen it done and believe me it's not nice). However, my mood is lifted considerably when I spot a piano and even more when we clock the outdoor table tennis. We could have some fun here but it is also my turn to cook and we have to make a dash to the shops to get some food in. To Rob's credit, he does like to cook and we have had some great meals, but today I just want to shower, eat and relax and not have to spend a couple of hours shopping and cooking up some gargantuan casserole.

After the shopping we also attempt to send a parcel back home with redundant bits and pieces that we no longer need and which only serve to weigh us down unnecessarily – things like maps and disposable cameras – but we leave it too late and the post office is closed. Thankfully, the guy who manages the gîte says he will send it for us in the morning. Shopping done and with a bit of time to kill I head down to the thermals to see if I can negotiate a spa bath or massage or anything that involves warm water and no walking. The spa building is a sizable place and from a distance reminds me a little of a railway station due to its length and the large arched windows that run along its side. The entrance is an impressive swathe of glass and coloured tiles and feels much more like a swimming pool or leisure centre, which it is in a sense.

Once inside the system is a bit confusing, but from the menu on offer I choose the basic spa bath treatment. The place is run by a collection of rather large and formidable women and through a combination of pointing, gesturing and goading I find myself naked, wrapped in a bath towel in a kind of chamber with a large bath-type thing in the middle. I didn't think to bring any trunks with me and to be honest I am not sure what the protocol here is, so I just stand there and wait for something to happen.

One of the scary women bursts in and tells me to get into the bath, which is slowly filling. I try to tell her that I have nothing on, that I am naked underneath my robe, but she just brushes my protestations away with a dismissive hand and indicates again for me to get in the bath. Oh well, I guess it's nothing she hasn't seen before, so I rather sheepishly take my bathrobe off and hastily clamber into the bath. She turns the taps on full, does another couple of things that I can't see and leaves. The bath quickly fills up and just as I start to worry about James Bond films my lady friend returns and turns off the taps and then leaves again. I lie there and just begin to enjoy the sensation of being enveloped by the warm water when suddenly there is a mighty blast of air in my nether regions. For a moment I wonder if my bowels have exploded, and the strong smell of sulphur doesn't help, but then realise that I am being pummelled by ultra strong jets of water that shoot out from different points around the bath. After a short time it really starts to become quite enjoyable and best of all is the powerful jet that pounds the back of my neck and shoulder region. I can feel the aches and tensions fall away. It's bliss. Even the acrid smell of bad eggs seems quite nice, in a volcanic kind of way. But all too soon my minder returns and I am told to get out, so I clamber out and find my way back to my clothes.

Refreshed and back at the gîte, I locate the kitchen and begin to knock up a turkey in red wine casserole. We eat well and later on I manage to have a little play on the piano until some miserable sod in the TV room tells me to shut up (I think – it might have been a request I suppose, but all I heard was some loud French shouting, which I couldn't make sense of). I miss the piano as I play all the time back at home and at times I acutely feel its absence. Rob's ukulele is great but not the same and my penny whistle doesn't quite do it for me (or I guess those around me). Jess is also a good musician, on both piano and guitar, and like myself has a natural improvisational knack for picking up new instruments: we have fun playing together.

We mooch around a bit, play table tennis with Craig and another guy who reckons he's a bit of a champ, although chump would probably be more accurate, and then as 10 p.m. beckons we head off to bed. Overall, it has been a positive day; although at times it can be a trudge, tedious and relentless, when the walking and scenery are good it can feel amazing.

DAY 23

BARÈGES TO LAC DE L'OULE

Today will be a long nine- or ten-hour stretch that takes us to an overall height of 2, 500 m – that's a lot of Box Hills – so we start early with my alarm set for 6.30 a.m. It goes off like a kick to the gut and I think I could easily pull my sleeping bag over my head, shut out the world and go back to sleep. But I force myself upright and give Rob a friendly shove. He has been muttering a lot in his sleep and last night it felt like I was sharing a cave with a bear that had gone into hibernation at the wrong time of year – lots of snuffles, snorts, bangs and thuds.

Breakfast is cereal, which makes a pleasant change, followed by coffee, tea and hot chocolate. Perhaps over the top, I know, but breakfast is the main fuelling up opportunity so we make the most of the good ones when they come along.

Rob is particularly unhappy with the map today and makes a point of trying to find out where we are and where we are going. I tell him that I don't really care where we are, let's just follow the markers and enjoy the walk, but I realise I am on a hiding to nothing.

After a couple of hours or so we have climbed up and out of the valley and into an amazing boulder-strewn landscape that once again reminds me of a set from *Star Trek*. It's beautiful today; the sun soon burns off the last remnants of cloud and we pass gorgeous lakes of deep blue water. Hitting a good rhythm, we leave Craig and Lucy for dust and when we hit an option in the trail we choose to take the longer, tougher route up and over the Col de Madamète. It's a killer 1,350-m climb but the views from the top are astounding. Whispers of cloud drift below us and the sun bathes the whole scene in a rich golden light. The fact that we have had to work so bloody hard to get to these places increases the sense of enjoyment and achievement a hundredfold.

After a breather and spot of lunch, we saunter downwards. Rob is forging ahead and seems a bit fed up, but that's probably because I beat him at table tennis last night. As I walk I think simple thoughts. I think about my breathing, my toes, the straps on my rucksack and how good my boots are. In fact, my boots are fucking great. Several hundred miles and not a single blister. For some strange reason I suddenly miss Bernard, our VW camper van. I don't know why it (he) has popped into my head like this, but I guess it is a symbol of home. In fact, we only bought the camper van four or five months ago so I am looking forward to a few holidays that don't involve walking. I wonder if we will ever make it to the end of this bloody walk. I think about where each foot is going so I don't slip and I think about Nicky and Jess and my promise that I will keep myself safe. We see an eagle today, turning slow circles in the warm winds high above.

It's a long, tiring descent but finally we get to the gîte, a place called Chalet Lac de L'Oule. The rooms are a little cramped but it's a nice place, right next to a dam, and after a shower we settle down to a good meal of rice and lamb curry washed down with a carafe of *vin rouge*. Rob cheers up and we play cards for a while.

DAY 24

LAC DE L'OULE TO AZET

There was a great thunderstorm in the night and I lay in my bunk watching the flashes of lightning through the dorm window. It was exciting but of course I hardly slept, and then was up at 6.30 a.m. The bloody alarm and getting out of bed is killing me. I am using my phone after my watch died ages ago and the alarm is a woman's voice saying 'It's time to get up; It's time to get up'. God I hate it – I hate her. The mornings are definitely the worst part of the day although, to be fair, this is generally the case for me, even at home. I don't like getting up early and these daily early starts are just compounding the feeling. The routine of up, toilet, wash, teeth, rucksack, feet and breakfast all seems to blur together in the haze of my mind. My feet, meanwhile, are definitely starting to look different: the veins are bulging on top and they have flattened out with my toes looking strangely angular. Will they ever be the same again? In the evenings I can't walk properly; I kind of lope around on the sides of my feet like a Neanderthal who's crapped himself. Not a good look all in all.

We leave at 8 a.m. and Rob, with a crafty bit of map-work, susses out a short cut. We make the relatively tiny climb of 350 m up to

Col de Portet in good time – in fact we are actually one hour ahead of Douggie Time, the first time we have ever managed to get ahead of the Great One. We both feel strong and energetic and we bound to the top with little effort. The early start really pays off and we realise how good it is to get most of the climbing done in the early hours. Once again we are above the clouds and the velveteen carpet stretches out beneath us. Rob stands back and takes a picture as I walk down the hill into the layer of cloud, disappearing into the mist.

In fact, it's a long and misty descent and feels quite eerie at times, like some kind of enchanted landscape. We walk through dewy fields filled with thousands of strange spider webs, ingeniously designed to trap their insect prey. As we walk through the water-laden, hanging cloud we can smell them. Amazing! We can actually smell the clouds. It's a kind of fresh, ozone-like smell. Puncturing the beauty of the moment, the toes of my right foot suddenly start to hurt; a stabbing pain like shards of glass in my boots. I guess it must be a circulatory thing and I stop and massage them and they begin to feel a little better.

The downward walk goes on forever, twisting its way steeply down through heavy woodland, but eventually we get to the small town of Vielle Aure. It's a nice place and we are there in good time so we stop for a Coke and hit the supermarket to stock up on supplies. We could stay here, but capitalising on our early start we decide to press on and head for Azet, which is about 500 m up the next valley. This will save us an hour or two tomorrow, which means we might even be able to do a double-stage and make up some lost time overall.

The climb to Azet is fine and the village itself is a small, sleepy place and seems pretty deserted. We have seen a few signs around for the Tour de France, which appears to be passing through this area in a few days' time, but at the moment it's deadly quiet. We eventually find the gîte and discover that we are the only people staying here: it feels strange to have the whole place to ourselves. Rob cooks up a tasty carbonara and we just laze around for a bit, playing the ukulele, drinking tea and pretending that we own the place.

Later on we search the village for a bar but the only place seems to be well and truly closed. Never ones to give in when in need of a beer, we knock on the door and a pleasant young woman opens up for us and lets us sit in their garden and have a couple drinks. I speak to Nicky and Jess later and they both sound good. Jess has finished school for the holiday and has done really well and I feel very proud of her. Nicky tells me she has been very organised and sent out the parcel with all our camping gear and maps etc., which we have planned to pick up in Luchon, the halfway stage of the walk. I tell her that's great and that we should arrive in Luchon in a few days' time.

'Err... Luchon?' she says hesitantly.

'Yeah, Luchon,' I say.

'Erm... I thought you said to send it to Luz.'

'What! You sent all our stuff to Luz?'

'Yes, I think so.'

'But we passed through there days ago!'

Shit, bugger and balls.

DAY 25

AZET TO GRANGES D'ASTAU

It is 6.30 a.m. and it's pissing down outside. I don't know what the date is but think it is either 18 or 20 July. I feel tired and fed up. Rob cooks up some scrambled eggs and mushrooms and then, after we have climbed into our Quasimodo ponchos, we head out into the bleak early morning rain. Neither of us is looking forward to today, seeing as we plan to join the ranks of the famous 'double-stagers' and take on two sections in one go, which all in all amounts to about ten or eleven hours of walking with some seriously steep climbing.

We stand in the rain on the edge of the village whilst Rob consults the 'useless' 1:50 map to check the right route. In front of us are three red and white GR10 markers pointing the way and I bravely suggest that maybe we should try following these. Rob makes a comment about me just 'charging off' in any direction I feel like and adds that the markers are unreliable and we have to go by the map. I feel annoyed and think of several somewhat uncharitable acts that could be undertaken with the bloody 1:50 map, mostly involving dark smelly places. For the last few days I have been especially observant of the GR10 markers along the way and it seems clear that the majority of these stages can be done purely by the markers alone. In fact, it seems to me that you don't need a bloody map to do the GR10 at all. I contemplate mentioning this to Rob but his beard and beret give him something of an austere look. Now, of course I do realise that all the literature and associated prevailing wisdom on the GR10 state that you need to have maps and compasses, etc. and that I am probably being a little silly about this.

All in all I am amazed at how well Rob and myself have got along and I guess it is no surprise that there is going to be some kind of issue that crystallises a degree of conflict between us; and to be honest, if it is just the map thing then that's pretty damn good going. I mean, Rob could have taken to me in the night with a crusty baguette (not in a sexual way I hasten to add) or tipped me off the Chemin de la Mâture or indeed just left me behind in Borce when I was faffing about with my little heart-attack episode. I know, of course, how important the maps are and I think I am probably just being slightly contrary in response to Rob's keenness to use them, so we both simply have adopted positions at different ends of the map continuum, so to speak. I guess it is relatively safe territory for us to express a bit of conflict. Also, I have conveniently forgotten that as well as Craig and Lucy getting lost on a regular basis and Corinne going walkabout, we also have got a little lost on occasions, so I know my 'just follow the signs' spiel is a lot of tosh.

We walk and walk and the weather is shit and for most of the day we can't see more than a few metres in any direction, being enveloped in a misty rain (there you are you see, no sign of the bloody markers – map and compass very useful… humble pie, anyone?). We climb about 1,200 m and although we have climbed higher this feels like the hardest bloody ascent so far on the walk. It just feels like it will never end and each time we think we have reached the top a new peak looms large in the mist. It's relentless and my feet, for the first time, are wet, sodden and drenched and I feel let down by my boots with which I have, to date, had such a good relationship. I complain to Rob about them and ask him if it's normal to get wet feet. The stupidity of my question surprises even me but I have come to expect that my boots will protect me from everything and that they are totally impervious to all elements, as if they have a little micro force-field around them. They squelch now as I walk along and I feel miserable and pissed off and think about giving up and going home (as I do most days), but I also know that I can't bear the idea of people thinking of me as a quitter. My feet have become strange alien things and they hurt in all kinds of ways.

Later, we have lunch – pâté and bread – in one of the tiny walkers' *cabanes* that occasionally sit along the route. These are little stone huts, maybe with a bed and fireplace, and most carry evidence of use from previous occupants, e.g. old tin cans, matches, condoms, syringes (OK, I might have made up a couple of those). They are dank and smelly and I can't say I would really fancy spending the night in one of these places. I think about what it would be like to get trapped in here with some kind of psychotic murderer, but then that's the way my mind works.

On the way down we meet a guy from Quebec who is doing the GR10 in the opposite direction. Bloody oppositional Canadians! He talks about football and tells us that he likes to put his 'tent up in a bush'. Rob and I exchange glances, in a spot-the-euphemism kind of way, and silently agree that we should perhaps move on. He wants to stop and chat about all the different walks he has done but I am freezing and soaked through and just need to keep moving to prevent myself from totally seizing up. For some reason I think this guy should 'get a life' and take up a more sociable activity. Hmm.

We finally get to the Auberge D'Astau about 6 p.m., drenched, knackered and with feet numbed by the wet pounding they have been getting all day. We book in and head for the shower, with its magical recuperative powers. It's impossible to find words adequate to describe the sheer bliss of stepping into the shower after ten hours on the trail. It's like liquid gold, an elixir, a heavenly rain that gives life to the nerve endings that have been gradually deadened through the combination of cold and lack of circulation. If the shower is powerful enough I direct it at my feet and just let them soak up the soapy warmth. It works miracles for the dreaded pancake foot. If it's been a hot day then the cold water is equally refreshing, washing away the sweat and grime and rejuvenating my spirit. I think it's safe to say that the shower is the real highlight of the day; ten minutes of total unadulterated pleasure. Are these words enough? Probably not. Let me just say this then: the shower is bloody fucking great.

The gîte is more comfortable than most and once again we get a small dorm to ourselves. There's a cafe next door and we tuck into the day's special of lamb and fried potatoes, which gives us a good and much-need dose of carbohydrate and protein, and to celebrate our first 'double stage' we order a litre of red wine. We soon start to feel human again and are also bolstered by the fact that tomorrow night we should reach Luchon, which is pretty much the halfway mark of our journey. When I call home, Nicky says she has salvaged the parcel crisis and managed to get it diverted or sent on to Luchon, so all looks good.

DAY 26

GRANGES D'ASTAU TO LUCHON

I am surprised to find that Rob is up before me. As I slowly and groggily open my eyes I catch sight of him checking the level of water in his bottle by using his finger as a dipstick. Something about the precision of his action makes me laugh; it's a little like someone checking the oil in their car. It's still pissing down outside and to make matters worse we have an extra-crap breakfast of bread so stale and dry it just dissolves into a pile of crumbs on the table. It's all I can do to stop Rob from hunting down and killing the manager of the gîte in what would be a terrible and tragic case of breakfast rage.

Today's journey takes us to the symbolic and much-anticipated halfway stage of our great trip and more importantly a rest day, which I think we both need. We've got a 1,200-m seven-hour walk to get there – and that's in Douggie Time, which means it's going to be more like eight or nine hours. My boots are still drenched from yesterday and it feels particularly unpleasant to pull them on over my nice dry socks. We stand in the doorway, ponchos on, each reluctant to commit the first step towards what is guaranteed to be a miserable, soul-destroying day. There's no through road here so the option of hitching or getting a bus is zilch and there's no doubt we would have taken it had it been there. Eventually we bite the bullet and set off and the initial climb up to the charmingly named Lake D'Oô is not too steep, taking us up through woods that at least provide some cover from the rain. The lake is lovely, with a 273-m waterfall at one end and a dam at the other, and a basic-looking refuge sitting right at the lake's edge. If the weather was a little better we might have hung around a bit, but as it is we push on.

Despite the rain I'm feeling OK physically, but the last few hundred metres of the ascent seem to go on forever. The rain stops and starts; we are enveloped by dense mist and cloud and the visibility is terrible. At one point the mist clears for a moment and we hear a strange skittering sound and look up to catch a brief glimpse of a couple of antelope-like Pyrenean chamois (or *izards* as they are known locally) racing away across the rocks. They are distinctive, with their small, pointy horns and like most things on four legs around here it seems they are hunted with some relish. As we reach the top of the first climb we hear distant rumblings of thunder, ricocheting around the mountains like a great angry sky giant.

The stage today is unusual in that after the initial climb of 1,300 m there are three cols to navigate before we drop down steeply into Luchon. As we move over and down the first col, thunder and lightning swirl around us and we are hit with a freezing rain, which then actually does freeze and turns into an icy hail that pounds our faces and hands. My fingers are going numb with cold and I keep switching my stick from hand to hand so I can at least keep one hand hidden up my poncho away from the rain. We are both soaked through with a combination of rain and sweat but we try and pick up the pace as the thunder rattles around us.

For the first time, I get a little anxious about the conditions. Here we are at almost 2,500 m high in the Pyrenean mountains in the middle of a massive electric storm hours from anywhere and not another person in sight. A little slip would be all it would take; a broken ankle or just a sprain and we'd be stranded out here, exposed to the mercy of the elements. It's a reality check, that's for sure, and matters are made worse when I admit to Rob that I jettisoned my safety blanket weeks back. He's angry with me and to be fair he's right. His mantra – 'Never take risks with mountains' – echoes around the valley and I feel a little foolish.

We are both so different: me with my laissez-faire, casual attitude to the whole thing and Rob with his sensible, safety-conscious approach. He accuses me of not keeping my promise to Nicky and Jess (to keep myself safe). How can I promise such a thing when I'm skipping along 2,500-m ridges in a lightning storm, having dumped everything remotely connected with personal safety, with only a tin whistle and a harmonica for protection? My argument is that we're on the GR10, a major walking route; if we slipped and injured ourselves someone would come by sooner or later. It's a weak argument and Rob just harrumphs and glowers at me and picks up the speed. Of course, he's still mourning the loss of his Dark-Eyed Girl, which doesn't help. Thinking about it, my tin whistle and harmonica probably make very good lightning conductors, so they won't protect me too well – but at least I will sound good as I get fried.

It's a cold, wet trudge downwards as we approach Luchon. We are totally drenched even with our ponchos on and our feet squelch with each step. It reminds me once again of the school sponsored walk I did with my mother all those years ago. According to

Douggie there is a chance that we can take a cable car from Superbagnères, the ski station, down to the town and all in all this would save us a gruelling 1,100-m descent of serious steepness and probably a good three hours or so. We finally approach the cluster of ugly cables, pylons and associated ski paraphernalia and pray that the cable car is still running. I've convinced myself that they must have stopped by now; that they would have seen us coming and packed up for the day and that we are going to have to walk for another miserable three hours. But as we get closer we hear the whirs, clicks and rumblings of machinery and finally see the car itself rising up out of the clouds like a heavenly angel coming to greet us.

The car gently glides into its docking station and the feeling of joy and relief surges through our bodies like some kind of euphoric drug as we realise that we are about to be whisked away from this cold, wet nightmare of a day. God, I've never fallen in love with a bit of steel and a few cogs before, but then there's always a first time.

We are unsure of the relevant cable car protocol, and to be honest don't care too much, and so, ticket-less and despite the attendant standing purposefully nearby, we climb aboard and collapse into the seats like a couple of rain-drenched rag dolls. We half expect to get thrown off but the attendant ignores us, either through pity or disdain, and the car gloriously sets off downward through the clouds and begins its descent to Luchon. Rob starts taking his clothes off but after a moment's initial alarm I realise he is simply getting some dry stuff on before we emerge at the bottom. I'm not quite that organised but manage to get my poncho off and change my sodden shirt. The car glides effortlessly downwards and the thought that we are doing in ten minutes what would normally take a few hours is pure heaven. Our pleasure is increased tenfold when at the bottom we clamber out and saunter off without having to pay for a ticket. Hey, we jumped the Luchon cable car!

It's a bizarre feeling to suddenly emerge onto the bustling streets of Luchon. It's like another world and suddenly the misery of the last eight hours seems a distant dream. First things first, we find a cafe and indulge in a large hot chocolate. Slowly, life and warmth seeps its way back into our ragged bodies and we hunt around for a place to stay. It's a rest day tomorrow so we are de-mob happy and after a few false starts we get a room in a good hotel called Le Bon Accueil.

After the usual shower and general recovery routine we have a meal of *confit du canard* and *frites* in a nearby place called the Bellevue and then head out for our rest-day drinks session. We end up in a basement bar that seems to be the one and only happening place in Luchon. It's full of cool young people smoking and sipping interesting looking drinks and I am not quite sure what they make of these two old bearded blokes propping up the bar and ordering a non-stop supply of beer. We even splash out on a packet of fags and generally drink ourselves into a stupor whilst the youngsters whirl around us. Stumbling back to the hotel I think to myself that these rest days are really actually quite bad for me. I'd be better off walking.

DAY 27

LUCHON

I wake up feeling terrible. We head out and get a croissant and some coffee at the Bellevue and Rob's vulnerable heart is once again captured, this time by the delicate beauty of our waitress. Over the course of the day we establish base camp at the Bellevue, sipping wine, beer or hot chocolate, and Rob indulges his growing fantasy to the extent that he even throws in the towel on our beard competition and has a shave and haircut at the coiffeur around the corner, in the hope that this might help to lend him a place in her affections. Over time Rob actually gets around to saying hello to her and it turns out she is called Celine, no mere waitress but the daughter of the Bellevue's owner. She goes to university in Toulouse and hopes to move to Paris, but the devastating news is that she has a fiancé. Rob takes this well and still feels that he may have a chance in wooing her away from her betrothed. He is a few years younger than I am but all the same I feel he may well be a little old for Celine.

I resist the opportunity of a shave and haircut from the coiffeur, although the idea is tempting. Four weeks on and my beard has moved pretty much onto full maturity, but looks a little wild and unkempt. I suppose I could trim it up a bit but feel committed to my pledge to Nicky and Jess that I wouldn't shave until I reach Banyuls and even to have it trimmed feels like cheating. I have at least got past the itchy and scratchy phase though.

The Bellevue both beguiles and becalms us with its dreamy backdrop to the gentle passing of time and with its array of characters that drift in and out like extras in an ensemble film piece. The couple – he gaunt and esoteric, she once glamorous but now with sagging face and a wig that fools no one – are like 1950s' B movie stars living out their fading days in the make-do set of the hotel/restaurant. The fat woman with the bulldog face and the actual bulldog that sleeps under the table by her feet. The grizzly man, all stubble and roll-ups. And then of course Celine, with a smile that can knock out a man out from thirty paces. We learn about her father, a self-made man who walked across the Pyrenees from Portugal when he was fifteen years old and got a job washing dishes at the Bellevue. Twenty years later he bought the place and also owns a house back in Portugal and one up in the mountains. Our rest day passes in a haze as we idle around Luchon and ironically I feel strangely restless as my muscle-memory itches to slip into its familiar pattern of motion.

DAY 28

LOST IN LUCHON

R ob has suggested another rest day so that we can properly prepare for the challenging next stage of our walk through the Ariège, a much-less-populated and sparser region of the mountains without the villages and gîtes that we have become used to. I think the truth of the matter has more to do with the lure of the Bellevue and its siren in residence, Celine.

Rob takes up base camp again and starts to copy out sections of Douggie's book, planning our route over the next ten days or so. To be honest, I feel a little defeated by the exercise and can't quite see the point but then I'm the one who can't see the point in maps and who jettisons his survival gear before taking a walk in a thunderstorm nearly 2,500 m up in the mountains. I go to the post office to collect our precious parcel that contains our cooking gear, maps and other essential stuff for the next stage of the walk. It's not bloody there.

I gesture wildly and remonstrate with the poor postie at the desk and try to explain that the parcel accidentally got sent to Luz but had been re-directed by someone in England to Luchon several days ago and had to be there somewhere. I even make him go and look again in the parcel area around the back of the post office. He phones Luz and tells me everything has been delayed by the Tour de France that has snarled up all normal life in the area. Stupid bloody race. Come back tomorrow he says. I report back to Rob and we decide we will pick up the parcel first thing and then head off and camp for a few days and try and make up for some of the lost time. With this in mind, Rob decides it might be best to buy a small tent from a camping shop as even he is a little unsure about how we might survive with just the Basha for cover over the next stage of the journey.

Later, at the Bellevue, a large crowd has gathered to watch the cursed Tour de France on a big screen that has been set up outdoors. It is strange to think that the actual race is in progress not far from here. The wind is warm but with a biting edge and the commentary from the race fills the space around the bar and tumbles out onto the street. Waiters weave amongst the tables, depositing coffees and glasses of red wine as they go. I wonder if Luchon is an oasis or a form of entrapment. I feel dreamy and lost as we wait for this parcel that may never arrive. Luchon smells of coffee, cigarettes and pastry and is full of cyclists – all no doubt fantasising about their own part in 'Le Tour'.

The town is attractive, with one main thoroughfare and, much more than other places we have passed through, it sits wedged between looming mountains on all sides, which give the place a somewhat oppressive feel, as if it's closing in on you. The crowd in the bar are getting excited as the race nears the end of today's stage and the Dane, Rasmussen, is beaten into second place. A large woman dressed all in white is seated just in front of me and her excitement leaks out through little jerky hand gestures. A

DAY 28

round of applause breaks the tension as the French guy wins the stage and the large lady leaves to continue her shopping.

We eat again in the Bellevue tonight, Rob, myself and the lovely Celine who doesn't seem too perturbed by our continual presence. I have become rather partial to *confit du canard* but Rob has moved on to turkey gizzards with gusto, even though we weren't too sure what they were first time around. Later we go for a quiet drink and wile away a couple of hours of the Luchon evening. I am not sure this is part of the effect that the town has had upon us, but we have totally lost track of time. We don't know the date, what day of the week it is and we don't know what our roughly estimated arrival time at Banyuls might be. Nicky and Jess are planning to fly out to meet us in Banyuls, so we need to get a grip of this whole time thing. I draw out a calendar for June, July and August in my journal, so that we can get a handle on when we started the walk and when we might be likely to end. It's weird how we can lose track of time like this. Are we losing our grip on reality?

169

DAY 29

STILL LOST IN LUCHON

No bloody parcel. My 'friend' in the post office is apologetic and says it must be on its way from Luz and to try again later. I scan the parcels knocking around in the backroom, thinking it must be there somewhere and badger him to go and check again. I go in several times more over the course of the morning, looking out for any signs of delivery and each time I catch him initially trying to avoid eye-contact and then giving me the Gallic shrug-off and a hopeful smile. I retaliate with my best Jewish shrug that probably signals something like casual desperation, if such a thing is possible. Can a Jew out-shrug a French man I wonder? That's a question for another day perhaps, or the basis for a very bad game show (a number of contestants get points for the quality of their shrug, i.e. range of facial expression, shoulder movement, hand position, quizzical eyebrow, etc. and are slowly whittled down to the final two who then have to go head to head with a – wait for it – 'Shrug of War'. I might have to pitch this to Channel Five when I get back).

Anyway, enough already. Rob and I agree that we will have to stay on one more day to see if the stuff arrives but then, if it is not here tomorrow, we will just have to buy the minimum equipment that we can survive with over the next few weeks and hope for the best. As I prowl up and down Luchon high street I find myself obsessively looking out for anything that might be a delivery van and following its progress to see if it is going to the post office, like some kind of weird postal stalker. Jesus, I need to chill out about this but I am desperate to leave.

It feels like all the momentum of our walk has been lost and Luchon has become this strange, transient netherworld, like one of those alternate realities from *The Outer Limits* or *The Twilight Zone*. For so long I dreamed of reaching Luchon. Long before we had even set off, this town represented the magical halfway point for us, a symbol of achievement, but now it's become my potential nemesis and drains the energy from me. I begin to fear that we will be trapped here forever, fated to see out the end of our days in the Bellevue and become more than just walk-on parts amongst the strange assortment of characters that we have observed over the last couple of days. It also looks like we will struggle now to keep to schedule and will probably have to cut out some sections of the walk to get to Banyuls in time.

DAY 30

LUCHON TO FOS

I go to the post office first thing whilst Rob settles in at the Bellevue for a coffee and a chat with Celine. As I tentatively poke my head inside the post office, hardly daring to catch the eye of my friend, the handful of staff at the desks break into a round of applause and a few half-hearted cheers. My man gives me the thumbs up and gestures towards a parcel lying on the floor behind him. It's arrived at last. With a vigorous and heartfelt shake of the hand I accept possession of the elusive package and head out, hoping never to see Luchon post office again.

Back at the Bellevue we have a coffee and with some excitement rip open Nicky's parcel that has been undertaking a little trek of its own around the Pyrenees, in the slipstream of the Tour de France. We find all sorts of goodies: maps, camping stove and assorted camping paraphernalia, new insect-proof pants, a hat for Rob, sweets and also the results of the final assignment for a course I had completed not long before we left. I passed.

It's time to leave Luchon.

Being stuck in one place has robbed us of our momentum and it's hard to get going. Rob seems quite low and given the opportunity would probably end his days at the beguiling Bellevue, which he has wrapped around himself like a warm duvet. We tentatively agree a plan that involves getting the bus to the next stage of the walk, a little place called Fos. Somehow, we both realise that we are never going to be able to walk out of Luchon; that we need to be pushed out, propelled like cowboys being thrown out of a sleazy saloon into the dusty street. Rob reckons we have time for a final lunch and so we sit and eat and say our farewells to Celine, who takes photos of us and showers us with her fresh-faced beauty. Perhaps it's not the Bellevue but Celine that Rob is really so reluctant to leave.

Eventually, we get the bus out of town and, after about 12-km, jump off and hitch a lift to Fos with a sprightly old lady who drives in an even more sprightly fashion. Being in a car feels so alien that we just sit there, bemused and silent. I also feel very low. I miss Jess intensely, to the point that it feels like a physical pain deep in my gut, a constant ache. When I talk to her on the phone I don't know what to say; we just chat and I guess that neither of us says what we really feel. Neither of us wants to upset the other. I guess that Jess doesn't really understand why I should choose to be away from home this long; why would she?

I don't think I quite understand it myself. I can sense the tone in her voice, the anger that I could leave her and her mother like this, or maybe I am kidding myself with an overblown sense of self importance; delusions of grandeur perhaps. But seriously, the hardest thing about this trip is being away from my daughter. Not the walking, the climbing, the aching feet, the pains – it's missing Jess. It feels like I am missing a part of myself and although I tell myself again and again that it is just a matter of weeks it feels like an eternity. I hope she will understand one day. Separation is also about reunion and what keeps me going on this trip is the thought of seeing Jess and Nicky again: it drives me forward. I feel continually guilty about being away, but perhaps that is how it should be.

Fos is a small, fairly non-descript place, although I kind of like it. The village gîte is fine and has a good little kitchen, so we cook ourselves some food after our tough day of sitting in a bus and a car for an hour or so. There is a little bar down the road so we drown our respective sorrows with a beer and try to throw off the sense of gloom that hangs in the air. Pictures of bears adorn the walls of the bar and we consult with Douggie to discover that we are now officially in 'bear country'.

The story is that back in the mid 1990s a few Slovenian brown bears were released into the wild just above Melles, which we will be passing through tomorrow. Seemingly, the project didn't go too well because the bears took to the sheep in a not very kindly way, which then, of course, left the farmers to exact their own revenge on the poor hairy Slovenian immigrants. French farmers will shoot anything, sometimes themselves, and so any opportunity to go on a bear hunt, justified or not, was not going to be sniffed at.

All this is slightly ironic, as the bears were re-introduced in the first place to replace all the poor indigenous bears that were more or less wiped out by hunters who saw bear-hunting as a fun sport up until the turn of the twentieth century. By the 1950s they were practically extinct. According to local folklore, one infamous hunter called Bonnecaze de Laruns killed fifty-five over the course of his lifetime. So there you have it, the brown bear wiped out not once but twice; Farmers 2–Bears 0. Anyway, it seems there are perhaps a handful of bears roaming around in these parts, which is quite exciting.

The other interesting, but not quite so exciting, thing about this area is the presence of the *pastou* dogs that guard the flocks of sheep high up in the mountains, like the one we saw back near Sainte Engrâce about two weeks ago. These are large white Pyrenean mountain dogs that not so much herd the sheep but live with them, their presence acting as a deterrent to any danger. Apparently, they more or less fell out of use at the end of the nineteenth century but, with the re-introduction of the aforementioned bears and the odd wolf or two, these huge monsters of dogs came back into fashion. The dogs are born in the sheepfold and quickly separated from mother and siblings so that they bond fully with the sheep; living, eating and sleeping with them. Essentially, they become part of the flock, alert to any danger and willing to see off, physically if necessary, any potential threat.

Around the village we have noticed a couple of large signs warning walkers about the *pastou* so I gently remind Rob of his duties as my official canine guardian. He doesn't seem to take them quite as seriously as I would like him to, and so it is with weary thoughts of bears and giant dogs that we head up to the dorm to crash out.

DAY 31

FOS TO REFUGE DE L'ÉTANG D'ARAING

The moment has come where we have to divide up all the extra camping gear that Nicky sent (and the small tent that Rob bought in Luchon) and, all in all, my rucksack has doubled in weight. Over the last few weeks I have carefully been getting rid of all possible expendable items from my rucksack in a bid to reduce its weight and I feel I have got to the point where the two of us have finally bonded. Now, with the extra weight it feels like I am right back to square one and I feel pissed off about the camping thing and having to carry all this damn stuff. I feel gutted and curse Rob silently (and of course unfairly and irrationally) for this whole camping malarkey. Rob bears the extra weight like a cross upon his back, saying that we just need to get used to it and get on with it, but silently I whinge to myself pathetically.

To make matters worse, having tried out my new triple g-force rucksack, I slip it off my shoulders onto my bed and crush my mobile phone that had been lying there innocently. The screen is cracked and I can't read or send text, although it remains just about useable for making calls. Jesus fucking bollocks and shit! How bloody stupid can I be? Already pissed off and miserable, I now feel gruesomely depressed. The phone has been my link to home and now that link has literally been broken in a moment of stupidity. I push the screen and a weird liquid pattern spreads across it, like a psychedelic map of France. I simply can't believe what I have done.

To make matters worse, according to Douggie we have one of the most serious and steepest climbs so far (around 1,500 m): and so it is with heavy hearts and even heavier rucksacks that we lumber out of Fos. Rob is feeling low and heavy-legged and seems to have very little energy, and our progress is slow. I feel low but OK physically.

Initially, it is a tedious road walk out of Fos and though Melles, a quaint little hamlet of a place. Eventually we get off the road and onto the path that leads up through the surrounding forest. This part of the track is a killer and, according to Douggie, consists of 1,000 m of ascent in the space of around 3 km, so we take small, slow steps to manage the steepness of the climb. On our way up we encounter a French girl, who we later establish is called Clare. She is also camping and carrying a vast rucksack that makes us look like lightweights. It turns out she is doing the second half of the GR10 after doing the first half previously, and we dove-tail with her as we make our slow, tortoise-like way to the top.

The walk is as gruelling as it gets but finally it begins to flatten out as we come across a small hut called the 'Cabane d'Uls' that sits at 1,868 m. Exhausted, we take a break and tuck into some chocolate, cheese and apricots. Refreshed, we head south-eastwards and, after a further brief climb, drop down into a large, grassy bowl of an area; and then after another hour or so we arrive at the Col d'Auéran (2,176 m). This spot apparently marks the border between the Haute Garonne and the Ariège Pyrenees, another significant marker in our journey as we move from region to region, this time into the challenging wilderness of the Ariège.

It has taken us six or seven hours, but we finally catch sight of our destination, the Refuge de l'Étang d'Araing. In fact, it's impossible to miss it; a huge functional corrugated iron structure painted a vivid orange that stands out in the rugged mountain landscape. We call it the Refuge D'Orangutan but in all its dayglo austerity it's a good place run by some super-cool French folks whose simple existence makes me feel inadequate. They are the kind of people that we want to be with their youthful exuberance, good looks and obvious zest for life and adventure. Even as we arrive they are in the process of a getting a hang-glider back from lower down the valley after what must have been an earlier outing, and the refuge is dotted with photos of their exciting exploits around the world. Perhaps we all want to be someone else at points in our lives. Perhaps these cool refuge people want to be Rob and me. Hmm.

Rob is not feeling too good, fluey and a little feverish, and he doses himself up with Anadin Extra, his preferred drug of choice (I'm a Nurofen man myself) and we sit around drinking hot chocolate and taking in the view, which is spectacular. The refuge actually takes its name from the beautiful-looking lake that sits bellows us, the Étang d'Araing, which we are told is abundant with fish even at this high location. The lake is an impenetrable cold grey-blue and I guess is another of the cirques or corrie lakes that we saw earlier, great bowl-like features gouged out by glacial ice and rock all those years ago. The mountains rise up dramatically around the lake, grey rock with a patchwork green covering of grass, gorse and other vegetation. It is the scale of these scenes that is always so impressive and I feel small and insignificant.

As we sit, I slowly beat Rob into submission with a barrage of terrible jokes: nothing like kicking a man when he is down, but it is rare that I get such a captive audience. I am especially pleased with my range of Jewish jokes and I laugh at them heartily whilst Rob just gives me a despairing kind of haunted look. Actually, most people give me that kind of look when I tell them jokes. A big party of about twelve people are also staying at the refuge and making enough noise for thirty. I think they are German and they begin to conveniently meet the requirements of all my German stereotypes, but to my shame it turns out they are Dutch.

Our sometime walking acquaintance for the day, Clare, arrives at the refuge, although it transpires she is just stopping for a drink before setting up camp somewhere nearby. She is a hard core camper, that's for sure, and this immediately endears her to Rob. It also turns out she is carrying forty packets of dried soup. This is all she eats so, of course, she becomes Clare the Soup Girl. Inevitably, Rob begins to fall in love with her and so Clare the Soup Girl joins the Dark-Eyed Girl and Celine in a little fantasy *ménage à trois* that will no doubt keep him going for days to come.

After food and just a little wine it's another shared dormitory experience and I realise we have become rather spoiled. We haven't been in a big busy dorm for what feels like weeks and there is the usual combination of snoring, farting, wheezing and sleep-talking. Rob's sleep-talking is now pretty much a nightly occurrence, most of it undecipherable, but he does seem to be something of a tormented man during these long dark hours, waking up exhausted in the morning. Talking about it together, Rob develops this rather fantastical notion of his 'other life' – some kind of nocturnal alter ego. Not for the first time I tell him he needs a therapist.

DAY 32

REFUGE DE L'ÉTANG D'ARAING TO EYLIE

It's a short four or five hours today, which is a blessing because Rob still feels under the weather. It seems like he has picked up some kind of flu bug and he's drained of energy and not up to much. The Dutch group are up and about and still being very noisy. After our breakfast – surprise – of toast and jam we ask the kindly refuge people for a packed lunch, as we have not been able to buy any food for a while. Then, as we prepare to set off we realise one of the packed lunches has disappeared, much to our consternation. It is a tricky moment but through a subtle bit of detective work, forensic observation and casually placed questions we discover it was nicked, or perhaps accidently misplaced, by the young boy from the Dutch group. He gives it back when confronted (well, gently asked) and I don't think he meant it but it just makes me even more irritated with the group. I have no reason to feel irritated by them; it's just because they are there I suppose, a convenient container for all my misery and pent up angst. Not for the first time, I tell myself I need a therapist.

The walking consists of a 1,000-m steep descent, which is welcome after yesterday's gruelling climb; it still batters my knees relentlessly, although they are generally holding up well. Rob is having some problems with his feet, especially his toes, and now and again we stop so that he can give them a quick massage. We pass some old quarries and mines at Bentaillou and the remnants of rail-tracks and ironclad buildings lie derelict like old ghosts of a bygone age. We wonder how many workers must have been killed in this place all those years ago. In fact, above the main mine building there is a memorial stone dedicated to three electricity workers who died here, comparatively recently, in 1960. The site at Bentaillou is in fact part of the mines of the Biros valley, down here in this western corner of the Ariège. They were lead mines and it was the discovery in the 1830s of a rich seam of zinc and silver-bearing lead that brought something of a small scale gold-rush to this dramatic and, let's face it, not particularly accessible mountain region.

Looking at it now, it is a desolate, barren place but in its heyday in the early 1900s the mines employed up to 500 miners, with two schools needed to accommodate the 200 or so children of the mining families. Stepping gingerly through the site now the scene is hard to imagine; the miners toiling away in the galleries deep below our feet, the noise of drilling and explosives, heavy wagons being winched up the steep mountainside and the miners who had to battle for twelve hours a day not only with hard rock but with the perils of 'lead colic' and silicosis. In 1926 the zinc market collapsed and the mine closed, with many of the workers going on to work on the construction of a hydroelectric dam on the nearby Araing Lake, which continued up until around 1942. Hard times indeed.

We get to Eylie, a tiny place consisting of just the one gîte and a handful of houses clustered around aimlessly. There is no sign of anyone running the gîte and so we hang around outside, dozing in the sun. And of course, as expected, the Dutch group are there in all their noisy glory. Neither Rob nor I can be bothered to make much conversation, so we just play miserable gloomy buggers (no doubt fulfilling their own stereotypes of the English). To be fair, they do seem very impressed by the scale of our trek but they are far too smug for comfort. As we wait, a French couple turn up, also going all the way to Banyuls. The woman is nice but he's a bit of a wise guy, a little arrogant and always laughing at his own jokes (which, of course, I would never do). Wise Guy tells us that they are aiming to get to Banyuls in about ten days time, but they are really going to have to shift to do that, doing double stages all the way.

Eventually, we get let in and after sorting ourselves out we go and eat in the home of the folks who run the gîte. It's like a homely kind of restaurant and whilst the food is good the conversation is a struggle. I ask our hosts if there is a phone box nearby, as my poor excuse for a phone has now run out of credit and I can't see the screen (that now resembles a psychedelic light show) to top it up. They say there is one down the road, so after dinner I set out to find it: it turns out to be about 2 km each way and the phone box itself is broken. My broken phone is really pissing me off and I find myself obsessing about it, fiddling with it incessantly as if somehow I am going to magically repair the bloody thing.

Fed up, tired and phoneless I go to bed and we find we are sharing a room with Wise Guy and his girlfriend. It's only about 9.30 p.m. and the Dutch lot are still up downstairs and being noisy. Wise Guy suddenly goes up in my estimation when he yells down at them to shut the hell up so he can get some sleep.

DAY 33

EYLIE TO CABANE DU PLA DE LA LAU

We have a long seven- or eight- hour stretch ahead of us, so thankfully the breakfast includes a surprise croissant. In my obsession over the phone I cheekily ask our hosts if I can borrow theirs to call Nicky so that I can get her to top up my phone from home. They kindly let me and I make a somewhat frantic, hurried call home.

Rob seems to be getting some of his old energy back and is in better humour as his fluey bug is on the retreat. His feet are still causing him some problems and as we get ready to leave he spends some time trying to coax some life back into them. He then asks me, rather randomly, whether I would prefer to give him a foot massage or a blowjob. Judging by the state of his feet the second option almost seems preferable; but thankfully neither takes place. Fortunately, Wise Guy and his friend have left already, as I wouldn't want them to be getting the wrong idea, especially as the Vaseline is about to put in an appearance.

Overall, we are climbing about 1,300 m today, with a few ups and downs, but we both feel energised and altogether more cheerful. As we tend to bounce off each other's moods I think Rob's return to good spirits has also lifted my own. The path pleasantly weaves through first forest and then open, heather-covered hillside where early bilberries or myrtilles seem to be in abundance. There is a freshness to the air and a sweet scent rises up from the myriad of tiny flowers that dot the ground with droplets of colour. The path then steepens for the climb up to the Col de l'Arech, which takes us a good couple of hours. This is the first high point of the day and from here we drop down through a heavily wooded landscape that reminds me of a place called Glendurgan Gardens, in Cornwall. There is something prehistoric about the place, the vegetation and sultry heat that hangs in the air, trapped by the heavy trees. We keep an eye out for bears and both hope that we might see one, whilst also hoping we don't, leaving ourselves in something of a bear paradox.

An hour or so from the Col de l'Arech we pass a little *cabane* that apparently can be used as a rest place by walkers as long as it is not already in use by shepherds or hunters (walkers being quite low down on the priority list). Still, seeing what they did to the bears, I think we would rather keep our distance from any trigger-happy, shotgun-toting hunters. We walk fast today, both putting the inertia hangover of Luchon well behind us, and it is with a satisfying sense of exhaustion that we finally get to a flat area by a river that has good camping possibilities. Douggie says that there should be a small walkers' hut here called the Cabane d'Aouen, but all we can see are the remains of a pretty ugly concrete building, so our sleeping options are somewhat limited. So yes, this is it; we're finally getting to camp, and Rob is in his element. There are a few other tents dotted around and we spot Wise Guy and go and say hello. He is impressed, in a slightly condescending way, that we have covered the same distance as them, but all the same we chat for a while and he laughs merrily at his own jokes.

As we set up camp I generally follow Rob's instructions and dither around and get in the way. This is very much Rob's territory and I feel I should let him do his thing. He expresses his concern about the possibility of a bear attack. It's possible, I guess, but unlikely, so it's really a matter of whether we need to take any precautions in the night, so to speak. I do remember a close encounter of the bear kind many years ago in Yosemite National Park in California, when a bear came into the camp during the night and started banging things around; although, to be fair, they're a bit bigger over there. Everything is bigger in America: trees, burgers, trucks, canyons. Why is that? I guess it's a big country and they need to fill the space somehow. In fact, I don't know for sure that it was a bear as I didn't actually see it. For all I know it might have been Nicky going to the toilet in the night.

Anyway, Rob suggests we gather up everything that smells, i.e. food, soap, toothpaste, etc. in a plastic bag and suspend it 30 m up a tree a good distance away from where we are camping. I wonder if this is somewhat overcautious, given that there are probably less than ten bears in the whole of the Pyrenees and that no one has seen one for years. I add for good measure that they are probably terrified of humans, especially after most of them have been blasted to pieces by the farmers. Still, Rob's view is better safe than sorry and it's true that my own health and safety record has been pretty poor on this trip. So, in the end, we compromise and I tie our smelly stuff up in a bag and stuff it in a tree about 4 m from the ground and about 3 m away from the tent. Our pants and socks are in the bag and judging the state of them the bear is in much more danger than we are. It would be sad if the last brown bear in the Pyrenees was killed by the smell of our pants.

All in all, this first night of camping feels a little strange, being such a change to our usual routine. Rob knows it's not quite my thing but I throw myself into it the best I can. The tent that Rob bought in Luchon is tiny and we are squeezed in like peas in a pod. It's cosy, certainly.

DAY 34

TO THE CORRIE LAKE

Three hours' sleep and I feel like Mr Crappy from Crapsville. The worst thing about camping is always the morning: when you wake up cold, wet, miserable, dying for a piss and with the taste of grass in your mouth and a small slug attached to your foot. It reminds me of too many nights from my misspent youth. It's all the faffing about that gets me, the camping paraphernalia, the zips, wet socks and the constant packing and unpacking and stuffing things in a hundred different bags. So I can't pretend that I feel refreshed as we set off for what is probably about a five-hour day on the trail. Having checked the maps and consulted Douggie we have decided to head for an interesting-looking corrie lake in the glacial heights above. Rob likes a good corrie lake and it sounds like a good plan to me.

The walking is good and it really is pretty desolate in places in the heart of the Ariège. It is certainly much more of a grand, mountain wilderness and there is a wild, unspoilt and remote quality to the landscape. The sense is of being up on a high plateau and the sweeping, open vistas are a welcome change from the folds of valley and forest that have been so much a feature of our journey so far. Apparently, the Ariège has the greatest amount of prehistoric sites than anywhere else in France and there is something about the region that just feels very ancient.

As well as prehistory, the Ariège has played its part in more modern history, most notably as a secret escape route into northern Spain during the World War One. Its rugged inaccessibility provided good cover for not only hundreds of Frenchmen but also RAF and American airmen who had either crash-landed or parachuted to safety after being shot down over Nazi-occupied France. Indeed, there is now an official way-marked walk, Le Chemin de la Liberté (The Freedom Way) that commemorates these wartime escape routes into Spain.

There were several well-organised escape lines in operation throughout the war, at different points along the stretch of the Pyrenean border; for example, the Pat O'Leary Line on the Mediterranean coast at Marseilles and the Comete Line on the Atlantic Coast near Bayonne. But many other escapees, aided by these well-organised networks, were filtered down through France and into the central Pyrenees. From St Girons in the Ariège, now the starting point of Le Chemin de la Liberté, the escapees were passed across the mountains along a chain of local helpers who clothed, fed and hid them at some considerable risk to themselves. Many hundreds of men were 'smuggled' across the St Girons-Esterri escape route and, despite many other routes becoming increasingly dangerous due to a combination of German surveillance and French betrayal, the St Girons-Esterri route remained in operation until the end of the war.

Thousands of Jews also fled across the Pyrenees into Spain to escape Nazi persecution and deportation to the death camps, and tales are plentiful of French underground networks assisting Jewish families in their passage across the mountains in the harshest of conditions. One of the many stories is that of Varian

Fry, sometimes known as the 'American Schindler', who, in the face of the Vichy Regime, helped up to 4,000 Jewish refugees escape the holocaust by smuggling them across the eastern Pyrenees. Earlier there were those who fled northwards in *la retraite* (the retreat) of 1939, in which a mass exodus of over 500,000 republican refugees struggled on foot across the high passes of the Pyrenees into France as they fled the Spanish Civil War.

Certainly, there is a weight of history in these mountains and they have more than played their part in the tortuous struggle and twists and turns of human conflict. As we make our rather more benign way along this vast highland border territory, enveloped by the rich beauty and serenity of the landscape, it is impossible to imagine the desperate stories of trauma, tragedy and human suffering that must have been played out along the many paths that we are crossing now.

As we walk, Rob and I also recall another well-known crossing of the Pyrenees from France into Spain, that made by Laurie Lee in the winter of 1937 when, carrying a saucepan, a few books and his violin, he staggered through blizzard conditions to volunteer for the Republicans in the Spanish Civil War. We think it was probably further eastward that he crossed and Rob is keen to recreate Lee's journey across the mountains, although this might have to be an adventure for another day (but not in winter – what was he thinking?).

At one point, at the height of the day's climb, we see a small group of people standing around by a gate that we need to pass through to pick up the trail. I get there a few minutes before Rob and say hello. One of the group tells me that there is a dog on the other side of the gate, guarding the sheep.

'*Pastou?*' I enquire, trying to look calm.

'*Oui, pastou,*' he replies. Oh fuck, I think.

'*C'est féroce?*'

'*Huh?*'

'*Le chien. C'est dangereux?*'

'*Ah, je ne sais pas.*'

Then why are you all standing on this side of the fucking fence, I ask myself.

Rob strides up and I fill him in on the situation. 'Oh, OK,' he says, and walks through the gate and nonchalantly sets off across the field. I clamber after him, as my life is now in his hands, and no sooner have I got over the fence than the dog itself appears in front of me.

Now, in my mind the giant *pastou*, this monster of a Pyrenean mountain dog, was slavering wildly like the creature in *The Hound of the Baskervilles*, poised on its thick haunches to launch at my throat and tear me to pieces. In my mind, I stared the dog down, drove it into submission with my masterful control of the situation. In reality, I just stood there, waiting for Rob to do something. In fact, Rob just casually chatted to the animal and I thought for a moment he was actually going to sit down and start stroking it. He said it was just a mangy looking thing, after a bit of food and I could swear he started rummaging around in his pockets to see if he could find it anything to eat.

'Rob, let's get going shall we,' I hissed, making slight leaving movements. Rob of course kept it casual and we sauntered down through the middle of the field. Well, I didn't saunter, I walked quickly and very stiffly as if I had a red-hot poker up my arse and kept looking back to see if the dog was chasing us. Rob was just wetting himself laughing at the pathetic nature of my behaviour. Later I try to convince him that, in fact, I had the situation under control, that I had the *pastou* in the palm of my hand, but he just looks at me quizzically and calls me a nobber.

We find the corrie lake, officially known as the Étang d'Ayes, and camp in a beautiful spot just overlooking the water. The lake is still and deep and sits in a perfect glacial bowl, the lip from which the river of ice once carved its slow passage downwards, scraping the rock clean. Strangely enough, the word 'corrie' comes from the Scottish Gaelic *coire* meaning kettle, which brings us back to our old friend the *bouilloire* (the French kettle where Rob keeps all his *sangliers*). Whatever, Rob loves the kettle lake and even whips off his clothes and goes for a swim. In the descending mist, as he squats down by the edge of the water before plunging in, he reminds me of Gollum from *The Lord of the Rings*. Ah, my precious.

We cook a tasty meal of pasta and even manage to have a little fire. Rob fantasises about Clare, his soup girl, and we wonder if she is camping nearby. We are low on water and don't feel we can quite trust the little stream that feeds the lake, as there might be cattle or sheep further up the line, so for the first time we crack open the iodine tablets. The water, although purified, tastes disgusting but hopefully is less likely to kill us than dead-sheep flavour.

As we prepare for the night, Rob tells me he is going to have a bivvy. I'm not sure what he means. Is it something rude? Should I look away? Does he mean bevvy? Turns out he means a bivouac and with our walking sticks and a bit of string he turns our two capes into a makeshift open style tent. It's very impressive and I reckon he is not far from squeezing fresh water from a rock and knocking up an *izard* skin coat. His head sticks out one end of the bivvy, open to the night sky but he's happy and, to be fair, I'm happy too as I have the tent to myself. As the night draws in a veil of mist descends and sits over the water like a wispy, ethereal hat. It truly is a magical place.

DAY 35

CORRIE LAKE TO SEIX

Rob can't resist having another swim in the lake first thing this morning, whilst I knock up some breakfast. The clouds hang over the rocks above the lake and then disappear, blown away in the breeze until new clouds come in and take their place. We have an easy downhill walk today and even take a good Douggie short cut that must save us at least an hour or two. Apparently, this section of the route can be treacherous in bad conditions, if the weather is wet or stormy, but it seems fine to us as we dip down from the high peaks and back below the tree line.

Soon we hit a main road that leads down to our destination, Seix (pronounced, unfortunately, as 'sex'). Rather than continue walking the last few hours into town we decide to see if we can hitch a lift, but there seems to be an almost total lack of traffic. To wile away the time between cars we play cricket, using stones and my trusty walking stick. Rob bowls some good deliveries, getting a decent bit of turn off the rough ground and even a bit of swing in these heavy mountain conditions (or more likely because he is just chucking a lumpy bit of stone at me). I can't hit a thing – so no change there then – and this doesn't bode well for our annual charity cricket match at the end of the month, when Rob and I lead opposing teams into battle for what has become something of an epic grudge match.

Bored, we give up hanging around waiting for a car to pass but as it is, the walking is great, easy and relaxed as we stroll along the side of the valley following the course of a small river as it tumbles downwards. We make stupid jokes about Seix, like errant schoolboys, but it keeps us going for a while. On the way we pass a lovely looking place called the Gîte d'Esbints, where pot belly pigs snuffle around rather engagingly amongst the bohemian surroundings. We are tempted to stop here for the night but instead just have a break and a drink before continuing on to Seix. The two main reasons for this are the chance to get our clothes washed and the fact that I can get a bus from Seix to the nearby town, St Girons, to buy a new phone. Also, and to my shame, I have cajoled Rob into agreeing that we treat ourselves to a night in a cheap hotel, wimp that I am.

As we walk through the outskirts of Seix we think it looks a little dull for a place with such a great name, but as we get into the centre realise that it is an attractive and happening little place that is high on both of our lists of 'Places We Would Like to Live'. We find an auberge run by some friendly Dutch people that only costs €35 and they will even wash our clothes for free.

We have a shower and a lie-down but when I take my boots off the pungent smell of my socks almost makes Rob pass out. He's got his head out of the window and is gagging, perhaps a little dramatically, but it is true that the smell is awful. I take our clothes down to the woman at the desk and apologise for the noxious fumes emanating from the plastic bag. I guess she's used to it. I also realise that I haven't exercised my bowels for three days; that's what camping does to you.

We eat downstairs in the auberge's restaurant and then go for a few beers in a bar after a walk around the village. In one end of the bar, a woman is giving a slide show lecture on the flora and fauna of the Pyrenees to a small group of semi-interested-looking people. We don't join in, preferring just to veg-out in the chairs outside, but when her talk is finished I do go and ask her about the mythical desman, the one animal that we would love to see. She gets quite excited by our interest and shows us pictures, although admits to never having seen one herself in the wild. The desman is a small and peculiar aquatic mammal, a little like a web-footed mole, but they are rare and shy creatures that keep themselves to themselves. But who knows, maybe our luck will be in.

After one last stroll around the village to work off the beer and food we go back to our comfy beds and collapse. The plan tomorrow is for me to get the bus into St Girons, whilst Rob has offered to sew up my sleeping bag that has somehow got ripped along one side. He assures me is a dab hand with a needle and thread.

DAY 36

SEIX TO ST LIZIER CAMPSITE

Ah, it's good to wake up in a real bed, although somehow I never sleep any better. I leave Rob to his lie-in and head off to get the bus, picking up a croissant from the *boulangerie* on the way. This change of routine feels strange and it is odd to be catching a bus again after being away from civilisation for the last week. The last six days or so since Luchon have been very different, the fact that we are camping and having much less contact with fellow walkers along the way. It looks like we have left Craig, Lucy and Corinne far behind and I miss their camaraderie.

This section of the GR10, the Ariège, is much more of a challenge. It's hard to see how Corinne, with just her sleeping bag, was going to manage it; as for Craig and Lucy, there are not so many posh hotels, or restaurants for that matter. Basically, the first half of the GR10 is very much a stage walk, the routes in the guidebooks taking walkers from gîte to gîte, which invariably means that you are going to fall in sequence with your fellow walkers. This section is broken up, the gîtes are few and far between and the feeling is that the Ariège tends to sort out the hikers from the trekkers. I am still not quite sure what category we fall into at this point.

Sitting on the bus and letting myself be carried along feels great and to be honest, to be on my own for a couple of hours feels great as well: I guess Rob feels the same. The fact that we have lasted this long together with no major bust-ups is amazing and a credit to our friendship.

St Girons is probably, by all accounts, a pretty low-key, sleepy kind of place but to me, right at this moment, it feels more like a bustling capital city. It's certainly the biggest town I have been in since we left England. Its main claim to fame (apart from being the starting point for the aforementioned Chemin de la Liberté) seems to be that it is home to the cigarette-paper industry which, as a past aficionado of the roll-up, is moderately exciting. Still, I manage to calm myself down and go and have a coffee to prepare myself for mobile phone shop hell. These are the worst kinds of shops, except perhaps Argos, because in any mobile phone shop, the world over, you have to wait ages to be seen, it's always more complicated than you think and once in their clutches it is hard to escape. The thought of negotiating this transaction in French makes the whole thing all the more daunting.

I have been hoping that I could just get a cheap phone and stick my old sim card in; but of course in the end it is not as easy as that. I have to get the whole caboodle, new sim card and new number, hooked into the French network; but at least I walk out with a phone that works. Mobile phones – both a curse and a blessing.

I make my way back to Seix and we set off at 2 p.m. for what should be a few hours' walk to another campsite near St Lizier. According to Douggie, there is a GR10 variant that should save us a lot of time and get us to the campsite by around 7 p.m. To get to the beginning of the path we have a few kilometres of boring road walk and so we hitch a lift and then jump out where we think the path begins.

After walking up and down and not being able to find it we spot an inviting hotel/bar by a waterfall and we find ourselves lured in. The bar is run by a Dutch woman. What is it with these Dutch? They're everywhere. Well, one thing leads to another and several beers and hours later we stagger out, stick out our drunken thumbs and hitch a lift to the campsite. It's a good campsite and we both feel pretty chilled out, possibly something to do with our earlier beer consumption. We decide to celebrate our good fortune by buying some olives and cocktail sausages from the campsite shop. Rob decides he is going to 'bivvy off' again, much to the interest of the other campers.

DAY 37

ST LIZIER TO AULUS-LES-BAINS

Every five minutes or so in the lead-up to leaving for this walk, it was 'Oh, don't worry Dave, you'll soon get your mountain legs' or 'Once you've found your mountain legs you'll be fine'. I was starting to wonder what the hell these mountain legs were. Do I get them fitted in one of those specialist trekking shops?

'Ah mountain legs, sir? How would you like them?'

'Well, could I have the very long and extra springy ones if that's possible? Something like kangaroo legs would do nicely.'

Yes, well. Perhaps they were right because it does seem that I have begun to find those elusive mountain legs and the climbing really does feel easier every day. This morning's climb is very steep, a real stiffener of a climb, though it's only 1,000 m. Unfortunately, Rob has not found his 'mountain toes' and they are really starting to cause him problems a couple of hours into each day. To be fair, he does have somewhat odd-shaped feet and a large carbuncle that has to be levered into his boot, and that might have something to do with it.

Talking about boots, I love my Berghaus boots. I may have mentioned this already, but they have been a total dream with not a single blister over the last five weeks and are unimaginably comfortable. I'm glad I got that extra half size: I would recommend it to anyone doing a trek like this. The whole way along this walk we have met people with all manner of foot problems: blisters, Achilles problems, sprained ankles and so on. My Berghaus boots have been the best investment I could have made in this adventure. That's it – end of product placement.

The height of our climb today is the Col d'Escots and the place is dominated by the vast skiing structures and associated apparatus. The steel cables, pylons and winching machinery look harsh and out of place in the bright sunlight and large tracts of trees have been scraped off the mountainsides. And very incongruently, in the midst of all this, sits the Restaurant d'Altitude which, to our amazement, is open. This is a rare bonus and we have a refreshing Coke and a Mars Bar and sit outside in the hot sun.

The path swings, loops and undulates its way around and down the side of the valley towards Aulus-les-Bains, roughly following the course of the river as it tumbles downhill. We soon hit the tree line and disappear into the undergrowth, the shade a welcome relief from the heat of the sun. We both feel remarkably content as we stride along, and as we pass a tempting and accessible section of the river we decide to take an impromptu shower.

Stripping down to our respective underwear we step into the river and make our way up to a small waterfall with a readymade plunge pool. The sensation of being drenched by the cold, crystal-clear water is wonderful. At this very moment some other walkers pass by and do a double take as they see a couple of near-naked men cavorting in the river. However, rather than quickly passing by they are clearly rather taken by the idea and head into the river themselves. Hmm. What have we started?

After a few more hours and obligatory killer of a final road walk we arrive at Aulus-les-Bains, a small attractive town. As is often the way at this time of day, the hot sun that we experienced further up the mountains has now been replaced with a steady drizzly downpour. It's one of the strange things about this walk, the way we alternate between the weather above and below the cloud line, moving from sun to rain and then back into sun as we climb above the clouds again. Rob wants to stay in the campsite but I feel the need for a comfortable bed, so I decide to stay at the Gîte La Goulue, which for only €12 is only about four quid more than camping. This means that Rob gets the tent and doesn't have to do any bivvying and I get a comfy bed: everyone is happy. I head down to the campsite with Rob and whilst he checks himself in with the miserable sod at reception we also discover that the place has a launderette, which seems like too good an opportunity to be missed.

The rain tips down, and so whilst Rob gallantly takes on the task of washing the clothes I seek refuge in a phone box and manage to give my mother a call using an old phone card. These long-distance conversations are always strained and a little surreal, and in the midst of it she asks me if I have learned anything about myself during the trip. Sterling Christian and Quaker that she is, I think my mother has been expecting me to experience some kind of miraculous Damascian conversion or Pyrenean epiphany or moment of spiritual awakening. I would find myself, find God perhaps, and beat my chest and cry to the spirit of my lost father whilst being lashed by thunder and lightning; a little like King Lear except without the beard and the daughters. But hang on – I have got the beard and there is Jess I suppose, my little Cordelia. Perhaps, in my mother's mind, I am on a pilgrimage – or she is on it by proxy, through me.

So anyway, from the phone box in the pissing rain in a miserable campsite, whilst Rob sits waiting in the launderette, I try to tell my mother that it isn't really like that; that most of my thoughts on the trail are mundane to the point of dreariness; that for most of the time Rob and I entertain ourselves with stories about farts, poo, nobs, beards and cricket. I'm not sure that I really get the message across, lost in translation perhaps. But it's great to speak to her and to hear that she is well.

Washing done and distributed, I leave Rob at the campsite and go and check in at La Goulue. It's a great place, a huge old building that according to Douggie used to be a dance hall. It has a beautiful garden, there is a cool, laid-back feel to the place and, best of all, when I am shown to the sleeping quarters I have a gorgeous single room all to myself. Unbelievable! It's clean, tastefully decorated, comfortable – and all this for a tenner.

I go for a shower and once again there is a sense of cool luxury all around: soaps and shampoos ready for use, lovely tiled shower and washroom. I think about Rob putting up the tent in the rain on the campsite and experience a twinge of guilt, but then it was his choice. And so I have a long luxurious shower and moisturise my feet with some nice lotion that Nicky put in the package that we picked up in Luchon. Then I crash out on the soft bed and doze for a while, revelling in the strangeness of the experience.

Later, I meet up with Rob in the local bar where we have a beer and dine out on kebab and chips, which really does feel something of a luxury. It's pleasant, sitting outside and watching the local life pass, and when we are finished we say farewell, shake hands and go our separate ways, Rob to his campsite and me to my gîte. Like my little trip to St Girons, I think we probably both benefit from a bit of space to ourselves and we arrange to meet up outside the gîte in the morning. As I lie in the cosy bed of my very comfortable room, I think again about what my mother was asking me on the phone, about what have learned on this trip. I write in my diary.

<u>What I Learned in the Mountains</u>

The rhythm of walking, of moving.
Sometimes metronomic,
Sometimes awkward,
Sometimes fluid.
The body; the tweaks the aches,
The muscles letting you know when they have had
enough.
The physicality of experience – of the day to day.
Having to rely upon your legs.
Time slows down; time stretches.
Thinking in distance, height, hours.
Being outdoors – all day, every day.
Feeling enveloped by the environment.
The joy of physical exhaustion – sleeping at 9 p.m.
The satisfaction of exertion.
The mountains change and move.
The angles, the sun, the shadow, the water.
They rise up like sleeping beasts.
I've learned about a potential I never knew I had.
I've learned that dreams can become a reality.
I've learned about confidence.
To be in and deal with new situations every day.
I've learned that routine is destructive; it destroys the
soul.
I've learned about adventure.
I've learned about separation and loss and the importance
of family.

I've learned about being away from people I love.

I've learned about the edge of experience; the fringes of what I can tolerate.

I've learned about space and light.

I've learned the value of food and water – especially water.

I've learned that profundity is not always to be found in walking.

My thoughts trudge just like my feet.

I've learned that I am small and insignificant.

I've learned the value of a good shower.

I've learned that to be on the move feels good; to be still is to be stuck.

I've learned to move with the contours of the land.

I've learned that each step, every single step is important.

I've learned to be sure-footed.

I've learned that mobile phones are both a gift and a curse, mostly a curse.

I've learned the value of friendship and family.

I've learned about the fear of death.

I know this, not learned it, but know it more.

That Jessica is the single most important person in my life and that to be away from her has been like a physical pain.

I've learned that to keep moving keeps the black dog away – although it follows me.

I've learned why my father kept moving; because to stop is to become overwhelmed.

I've learned that a good sleep is as elusive as a bear in the Pyrenees, but certainly more welcome.

I've learned the value of hot chocolate.

I've learned about frustration.

I've learned that possessions are meaningless.
I've learned that I can carry everything I need on my back.
I've learned that some people are happier than me and some unhappier.
I've learned that some people have nothing and no-one.
I've learned that cities turn people into themselves.
I've learned that it is good to say hello.
I've learned about my feet.
I've learned how to walk.

So, I guess my mother might have been right after all.

AULUS-LES-BAINS
TO VICDESSOS

I wake up feeling good.

After making the most of the luxurious shower facilities available I go out to meet Rob at our rendezvous point outside the gîte. In the fresh, rainless light of the morning, Aulus-les-Bains reveals itself as a quiet place, sleepy and unremarkable. It's another spa town, as the name suggests, and like many of these spa towns it clearly enjoyed its moment of glory in the early nineteenth century and then slipped back into a drowsy rural tranquillity. Mind you, this town's particular moment of glory comes with something of a health warning.

In the 1820s, a syphilitic army lieutenant found relief in the waters of Aulus, most likely because they counteracted the side effects of the mercury that was used to treat syphilis in those days. As word spread of the 'special' qualities of the local water the town developed a rather infamous reputation and was frequented by so-called 'invalids of love', and 'young people with shameful illnesses', to the extent that by 1849 Aulus had three hotels, a nice new bridge and an avenue of inviting acacia trees to attract new visitors. With the advent of syphilis treatments that surpassed the waters of Aulus, the town rather wisely reinvented itself as a 'cholesterol spa'.

We go and buy ourselves some croissants from the *boulangerie* and have a quick blast on the Internet in the little library. It's funny, but I sit in front of the screen and can't think of what I want to do or write. I check my emails, which is always something of an anti-climax, although it is good to be able to send a message home. Being away from computers and emails for so long does make me realise what little value they really have, in the greater scheme of things.

In fact, I have reflected a lot upon the perils of modern life during this walk. We sit for hours, days, years, bathed in the electronic perma-glow of our companion computers; tooled up with blackberries, iPhones and all manner of gadgetry paraphernalia, and hooked up to Facebook and Twitter like some kind of social life-support system. Do these things bring us closer together or do they in fact alienate and isolate us ever further from the daily workings of human life? It seems there may be something of an irony in the idea of 'social networking', in the sense that we are only further losing touch with what it means to be 'sociable'. Technology, so it seems to me, ultimately makes our life more complicated, however well it is wrapped up and presented. And that's what this walk is all about in many ways: the beauty of simplicity.

Anyway, after faffing about with the Internet we are behind schedule and so decide to hitch the first stretch to save us some time, but after about half an hour with no luck we realise that we need to crack on before the whole day is lost. It has started to rain again and we are beginning to feel wet and miserable and neither of us is in a walking mood, but once we get going things feel a bit better. In fact, it turns out to be a good stage, helped by the sun coming out and drying off our damp clothes.

We make good time and, after carefully studying both Douggie and the map; Rob reckons we could cut out a big loop of the main GR10 and instead take an optional variant that will take us to Vicdessos and probably save us a day or two. Due to our couple of days lost in Luchon we do need to make up some time from somewhere if we hope to make it to Banyuls for 16 August, so all in all it seems like a good idea. After all, we are not GR10 purists. Our aim is to go from coast-to-coast and we are not going to beat ourselves up about a little short cut here and there.

And it does turn out to be a great day's walking, especially one section through a valley that is incredibly beautiful in all its rich, green abundance. We follow the course of a river along the valley floor and horses and cows peacefully graze on the lush grass. I do seem to be getting fitter each day now. Once or twice, as we walk, we see and hear large rocks tumbling down the hill towards the valley floor, I guess dislodged by heat expansion or the rain higher up in the mountains. We would have to be quick to get out of the way of one of these buggers as they come haring down the mountain slope. The other sound that we hear is the intermittent whistling of the alpine marmots as they signal our approach to each other. It's a warning alarm that sounds almost birdlike, and they follow our progress with a curious caution from the safety of their burrows amongst the rocks. In fact we rarely see them, very occasionally catching a glimpse of a cheeky face as it quickly ducks down behind the safety of its rocky hiding place.

We get to Vicdessos, a fairly functional kind of place, and make our way to the municipal campsite that is fine but very busy. Rob bivvies off again and we eat two large tins of ravioli. I'd forgotten how nice ravioli is and whilst wallowing in this pasta-based bed of reminiscence I tell Rob my dad's old ravioli joke: he just looks at me with bemused concern. Fair play, it's a bad joke. As we hunker down for the night, unfortunately I start to feel quite rough and it feels like I am getting a cold. I wake at 5 a.m. to a bad fit of coughing so knock back some Nurofen and eventually drift off back to sleep.

DAY 39

VICDESSOS TO SIGUER

We wake up at 8 a.m. and don't start walking until 12.30 p.m. It takes us a long time to get going and I feel frustrated with our late start to the day. The temperature is often hitting the nineties by early afternoon and we really need to be doing the bulk of the walking as early as possible, so that we are not climbing in the stifling heat. I am impatient to get going but Rob is struggling to get himself motivated. As we finally make our way out of town I am aware of a little tension between us and I find myself withdrawing into myself, fed by petty feelings of annoyance. I recognise that my tendency to withdraw and slip into a simmering resentment that just bubbles around uselessly comes possibly from growing up with a depressive father, who when angry just withdrew into himself, leaving his dark unspoken mood to permeate the house and family.

We have more or less lost a day and both of us are feeling a little fed up, although invariably the process of walking manages to dispel these feelings pretty quickly and by mid afternoon we make our way into a little place called Siguer, which sits at the foot of a deep valley. It's too late to begin another big climb, as it's going to be at least seven or eight hours until our next stop, so we decide to call it a day and hang out. Siguer is still and quiet with absolutely no life and it appeals to the hermit part of me. It's a place that you could just hole up in, shut away the world, and exist in blissful peace. Rob says the place is dead, really dead, and he can't see any of the appeal that I can. There's no shop, bar or gîte and the only place to stay is a small and very basic room that has been set aside by the village for walkers. It's damp, smelly and depressing but will have to do, and so we dump our stuff and just knock around, reading and sleeping.

DAY 40

SIGUER – CAMPING

A sore throat seems to be creeping up on me stealthily and there is a slight hangover from yesterday's little bit of tension, but after we start walking things soon get back to normal. Walking really is very therapeutic in this regard. It's a short but really stiff climb up to the top, passing through a little village called Gesties, which makes us laugh simply because it rhymes with testes. Our humour is slowly sliding further into the primitive recesses of our minds, that were once the preserve of the grubby adolescent (and probably, I think, even beyond).

We top up our water bottles at a precious fountain and then press on up a steep, narrow cattle-track that skirts around some woods to our left. The route is poorly marked and we have to stop now and again to get our bearings. Eventually we get to the Pla de Montcamp at 1,904 m and the landscape flattens to a great panorama, bleak and wild. It is easy to see why this stretch of the Ariège is seen as the most daunting section of the walk, and why many people call it a day at this point due to the lack of gîtes and the need to camp. Some walkers also skip this stage and pick up the trail later on where accommodation is easier. Water is scarce and I have to admit that Rob's map reading does come into its own as the route marking is often poor and we have to plan carefully where we can camp, the presence of water always being the first consideration.

Up until Luchon the presence of food and water was not something we had to question that much, the GR10 taking us through villages and into well-established gîtes, but up here in the Ariège it really is remote, there is nowhere to sleep at night but our tent and we can't take water or food for granted.

From the Pla de Montcamp we descend south-eastwards and the path is much better marked with the familiar red and white GR10 stripes daubed onto rocks along the way. At the Col du Sasc (1,798 m) we pass another shepherd hut, the Cabane du Besset d'en Haut, which could sleep about three people at a push, but we decide to press on and find a camping spot at the bottom of the valley. We pass a few more of these shepherd huts on the way, but none of them look too inviting, then we begin to make a long and exhausting descent through the valley, moving through the tree line and down into a wooded section that seems to go on forever. The path zigzags and we have to pick our way carefully among fallen branches, tree roots and rocks; it would be easy to trip or turn an ankle.

Finally, we get to the bottom of the valley, having taken about four hours to get from Pla de Montcamp, and find a good camping spot in a clearing next to the river and a small road. We stick the tent up, make a fire and have a feast of soup and pasta; and although it pains me to admit it, I am actually enjoying this whole camping experience. Any remnants of irritation that might have been hanging around between us have been well and truly blown away by the day's walking and we chat and play the ukulele as the day draws in around us. We meet a middle-aged woman sitting alone on a bench by the river and it turns out she is terminally ill and has come out to spend a few weeks in some of the thermal spa baths of the area, on the advice of her doctor. She is a nice woman and it is desperately sad to see her out here, on her own, facing the last weeks or months of her life. Even with our limited language, it is a poignant, sobering moment. I wonder what her story is. Does she have a family? Is she alone? It's an odd, brief encounter out here in the middle of nowhere and puts the trivial folly of our own journey into perspective.

DAY 41

TO THE REFUGE DE RULHE

I wake up feeling good and am beginning to come to the conclusion that I sleep much better when we camp. This is music to Rob's ears of course and he feels truly vindicated. Fair play to him. We get going in reasonable time but after an hour or so into the walk the gradient is so steep we are reduced to tiny pigeon steps as we make our slow and torturous way uphill. We've got a long day ahead, possibly a good ten hours, and it's a relentless upward hike all the way without any respite. As we consulted Douggie and the map before we set out we could only exchange glances and utter the words 'fuck' and 'bastard' in various combinations as we anticipated the day ahead.

The path is very overgrown at times and we have to push through head-high bushes and bracken to make our slow way upwards. At these points, when I know there are hours of relentless climbing ahead, I slip into a sense of dissociation; my mind and body separating out as I find ways of tolerating the pain, strain and tedium of the walking. My body becomes something almost robotic, mechanical, as I try to cut myself off from the demanding physicality of the experience and my mind drifts off to all sorts of places as a way of avoiding thinking too much about what it is I am actually doing. On the general scale of feats of endurance this walk is pretty low down, but it does make us think about how and why some people take on some of the extreme challenges that they do; what it is that drives them ever forward.

We have lost our erstwhile companions Craig, Lucy and Corinne, and although we may be wrong, our guess is that they had enough and decided to call it a day. As for Rob and me, although we have contemplated the idea of throwing in the towel at different points along the way, we can both be obstinate buggers and we have become somewhat fixated with reaching the end of this walk: the magical Banyuls-sur-Mer that sits like a pot of gold at the end of our tortuous rainbow.

Eventually the punishing gradient starts to drop off and we come across a veritable hive of activity that is the Centre d'Accueil du Plateau de Beille. It's a busy restaurant built for the skiing season but which remains open all year round for the walkers and day-trippers who venture up to these parts. There is road access, which explains the people, and it is odd to encounter such hustle and bustle after days of virtual isolation. The restaurant is like an oasis and we tuck into a Coke and Perrier Water each and even splash out again on a Mars Bar. God, this is the good life. The toilet is also welcome relief as camping has the same effect on my bowels as accidentally sitting on a tube of superglue, and I make the most of the situation. Relieved and almost childishly excited by my bowel activity, I start to tell Rob about it but like a traffic warden he holds his hand out to stop me in my tracks.

We see a man and young girl who walked past us last night when we were camping and stop have a bit of chat. He is a Belgian guy called Hans and is walking to Banyuls with his daughter, hoping to make it several days ahead of us. He does look super-fit, all muscle and wire, although we feel sorry for his daughter who is going to get dragged along in his wake. As they breeze past, Hans warns us of a storm ahead and suggests that we better get a move on if we want to get to the refuge safely. Blimey, and we've still got five or six hours to go.

Still, heeding Hans' advice we get cracking and the trail flattens out into an area that feels like a high plateau which makes for fairly easy walking. The race is on and Rob, using the map to our full advantage, spots a tiny short cut over the top of an outcrop that gets us ahead of Hans, who is walking without a map. Soon, the going gets tough again as we climb upwards to the Col de la Didorte (2,093 m) from where the route takes us up onto a high section of ridge walking. This is very unusual, as the trail almost always takes us up and over, from col to col, and it is a very different experience to be walking along the spine of this mountain. If it wasn't for the black foreboding clouds building up behind us we might have enjoyed it, but as it is we just have to, push on as fast as we can for fear of being caught out here, high and exposed, in an electric storm.

We pick the pace up even more and end up half walking and half running, as we skip, pick and thread our way along the ridge at a speed which is probably not that safe in itself. Hans somehow managed to get ahead of us again but we soon catch him up and we can see that he is being restricted by his poor daughter who is doing the best she can to keep up with the urgent pace of her father. Thunder starts to rattle ominously around us and we both start to feel really quite anxious that we won't make it in time and might have to take some kind of evasive action to prevent us becoming the dreaded toast and jam of Rob's worst nightmare.

After an eternity of exhausting skittering along the ridge we eventually see the refuge, like a mirage, in the distance. This is no dingy den of a place but a full-on modern mountain refuge and the relief that floods through us when we see it is palpable. We stop for one brief photo opportunity, wherein Rob writes 'beer' on a bit of paper with an arrow pointing at the refuge, and then hurtle down the hill whilst the storm begins to break around us. As we arrive, the edgy adrenalin of the last couple of hours transforms into warm relief and we celebrate our survival with a couple of immediate beers with Hans (and a Coke for his daughter) whose welcome advice saved us from a potentially dangerous situation.

The place is stunning, and at around 2,300 m is the highest point of our journey so far. The peaks of Andorra lie to our south and the mountains rise up around us, vast cathedrals of shattered stone that reflect the early evening light like great sheathes of grey metal. The storm doesn't quite break but the thunder ricochets and rolls around the mountaintops like a great giant pacing the heavens. We are also on an emotional high, more so because of the adrenalin-fuelled race to get here, and instead of eating in the refuge, which would be easy to do, we decide to savour the moment and cook our own meal, perched on rock like tiny, puny humans in a vast sea of rock and air.

After we have eaten we head inside and share a couple of carafes of red wine with Hans, who we like very much. Then we collapse into bed and although there are no independent lights in the refuge (one out, all out), not even my insomnia can prevent me from falling into a deep sleep.

DAY 42

REFUGE DE RULHE
TO MÉRENS

It's a reasonably short five- or six-hour stretch ahead of us today, but the weather has not quite recovered from yesterday's rumblings and the skies are grey and laced with a light rain. Despite being a shorter stretch than yesterday, it involves 1,500 m of descent, which is equally gruelling in its own kind of way. Hans and his daughter are up and out before us and it is easy to see that they might make Banyuls several days ahead of us.

After breakfast we head off, and following about ten minutes of picking our way down from the refuge we find ourselves in a vast landscape of enormous boulders, tossed around from aeons gone by. It's as if the great sky giants responsible for yesterday's storm have been entertaining themselves with a little game of rock boule. We spend our time leaping from one to the other, the correct term being 'bouldering' I am informed. So bouldering we go and it's fun to be jumping and scampering across the rocks, using our rucksacks for momentum, although now and again a step is misjudged and we nearly go tumbling over the side of one of the great lumps of stone. It is easy to become a little casual and a little reckless at these times; the possibility of serious injury never seems to be that far away.

After what seems like hours of bouldering we then hit the beginning of the 1,500-m descent down towards Mérens. As it happens, the descent is less challenging than I feared and as we reach the bottom of the valley, which flattens out along the course of a lively river, we are greeted heartily by Hans and his daughter, plus his wife and two other children, who are all tucking into a fine picnic laid out by the bank of the river. It turns out that his family have driven out from Belgium, found a place to stay locally and then walked out here and lain in wait to surprise the two of them as they walked down from the mountain.

Man, what about that! What a family! Not only that, but they invite us to sit down and join in their picnic, and so without a second thought we plonk ourselves down and tuck into a bit of bread, cheese and sausage. We like Hans and his family and decide that we could live with them if they decide to take us on as two surrogate and slightly feral distant relatives. But the offer is not forthcoming and so as a light rain begins to fall we thank them for the lunch and say our goodbyes.

We reach Mérens, a sizeable town that has a massive highway ripping through the middle of it, a main French–Spanish route, and we find a cafe to collapse in for a couple of hours and watch the juggernauts blast by like monsters from another planet. Being away from the general mass of humanity for so long has made watching these lorries feel a bit of a novelty, although to be fair it soon wears thin. Rob likes the eccentric cafe, run by an elderly Madame with a large beehive and crumpled fag hanging out of her mouth, a real 'Fag-ash Lil'. There's an English guy, an ex-soldier, also sitting outside the cafe and we chat to him a bit. It seems that he has a friend down here somewhere who he is trying to hook up with, but he seems a bit of a drifter and will just head off wherever his fancy takes him. As we wile away time in the cafe the rain is really starting to come down, so we decide to head for the *gîte d'étape*, 'Le Soula', that Douggie rates as being 'one of the best along the GR10', especially for its good food.

We're soaked through, knackered and a little fed up, and by the time we walk up the hill and find the place it's absolutely pissing down. There is no-one around but we find a little self-contained outer room with kettle and cooker that is obviously for walkers staying in the gîte, and so we make some hot chocolate and hunker down with a few other folks until someone comes and tells us what to do.

The gîte is a nice place, that's for sure, and about as far from you average bunkhouse as you can imagine. It's all tasteful décor and arty wall hangings and the beds are spaced out around the large house in their own little areas, so that there is a good degree of privacy. If anything, we feel a little out of place, like scruffy poor relations at a posh family gathering. Despite what Douggie says about the food we decide to save money and cook for ourselves in the little out-house. Later we buy a beer and make ourselves at home – as best we can.

I have adopted a little ritual every night of carving the passing of each day into the handle of my faithful walking stick with my penknife, as a prisoner might etch the passing days of his sentence onto the wall of his cell. This isn't to say that I am experiencing this walk as a prison sentence – far from it; I have been privileged to have been able to undertake this venture, in the company of a good friend and with the blessing of my family. But my relationship with the GR10 has certainly been ambivalent at times as my energy levels, both physical and emotional, have ebbed and flowed with the very contours of the mountains themselves. Exhilarating and mundane, relentless and surprising, I have at times both wanted it to end and last forever. And each night, after I have showered, eaten and gradually recuperated from the day's exertions, there is something gently reflective to be found in the act of carving another notch into the yielding, weary wood of my treasured stick. It marks the passing of time but also of a process, a journey, as I contemplate the days gone and the way ahead. My walking stick has become an extension of myself and I feel deeply attached to it.

DAY 43

MÉRENS TO REFUGE DES BÉSINES – THE EASTERN PYRENEES

It's still pissing down outside when we wake up. Rob gallantly walks down the hill to get some croissants (having decided to skip the house breakfast) and we eat them in the little out-house, washed down with lashings of hot chocolate. Our clothes are still wet from yesterday so we stick on what remaining dry clothes we have, pull on our ponchos and head out reluctantly into the rain. Leaving the gîte, the lane passes an ancient-looking church that has an impressive tower dating from around the eleventh century. The rest of the church, along with most of the village it seems, was burnt to the ground by Spanish bandits in 1811 – pesky bandits.

The path follows the upward course of a small but lively stream and the first couple of hours feel fairly easy. But then, as ever, the trail rises steeply as we begin the stiff climb up towards the high point of the Porteille des Bésines. Although on paper this is one of the shorter sections of the walk (around four hours,

Douggie Time), it still involves a climb of around 1,300 m, which is far too many Box Hills for my liking. But all in all, the climbing feels OK and the rain has eased off slightly, so that we get some respite from the elements along the way. We pass time by talking about farts, shit, sex and death, so make of that what you will, Mr Freud. Perhaps we are really getting down now to the essence of the human condition, or maybe that's the male condition. Stripped bare of all the usual accoutrements, the trappings and social paraphernalia with which we accessorise our daily lives, it simply boils down to the beginning, the end and the functions of the body in-between. It's a primitive view, that's for sure, but perhaps that's what happens when you take two blokes and let them loose in the mountains. Certainly I have a tendency towards the nihilistic and solipsistic, which is of course why I am so drawn to the idea of living in cave like a hermit.

Of course, take away any sense of value and meaning in life and despair will soon loom large on the horizon. Or perhaps given the right conditions one would eventually reach a point of emotional equilibrium, of balance and health. Maybe you need to pass the despair barrier before you hit the aesthetic heights of art, value, sense and sensibility. Blimey, I'm really prone to bouts of existential angst. But this is another interesting feature of this walk; the constant oscillation back and forth on a continuum between mind and body.

Talking of the body, I seem to be breaking wind with disturbing regularity, to the point that Rob has become wary of walking too close behind me for fear of getting a face-full of the noxious fumes. We decide I am suffering from a clinical condition, which we term Pyrenean Flatulence, and is probably the result of an overdose of soup and pasta. I develop a theory about variations in air pressure and the effect this can have on one's output of wind, but Rob thinks this is nonsense and he's probably right. Still, I am curious as to whether mountaineers fart a lot, as a general rule. Funnily enough, and to stay for a moment longer on this theme, there is a myth that the very verdant nature of this particular valley pass, an ancient trading route across the spine of the Pyrenees and into Andorra, is the result of being heavily fertilised by the sizable droppings of Hannibal's elephants in 218 BC. Well, it's a good story and somehow fitting, considering the present state of my own nether regions.

We make good time and reach the Refuge des Bésines in the early afternoon and decide to grab a bite of lunch and then press on to the Lac des Bouillouses. This would count as a double stage and according to Douggie is an option only for the 'super-fit', but seeing as we are behind schedule we think we may as well give it a go. However, as we get a drink from a bloke in the refuge, who resembles a one-eyed pirate, and sit outside to eat our bread and cheese, another big storm blows in out of nowhere and we decide we had better stay put rather than risk getting caught out again. It's frustrating, especially as it is only early afternoon, but it's a question of better safe than sorry and 'Old One-Eye' behind the bar doesn't help with his gloomy predictions of the weather ahead. It is amazing how these storms can seemingly appear out of nowhere and stories of poor trekkers being frazzled by lightning up here in the high mountains are not uncommon.

The Refuge des Bésines is a functional affair, all metal and hard angles, and sits at 2,104 m in a dramatic expanse of tree-clad grey rock. I am sure the views would be stunning if it weren't for the rain and clouds that hang heavily around the refuge. Our pirate friend has disappeared and the place seems to be run by an attractive young girl in her early twenties who turns out to be the most grumpy, miserable, sour-faced person you can imagine. Her potential beauty is marred by a constant twisted and resentful snarl that brings to mind the image of a lemon being stuffed up a cows arse. Rob quickly names her 'Little Hitler' and we make a bet to see who can be the first one to make her smile.

We wile away the afternoon whilst the storm knocks around outside by playing Rob's cricket game Owzat! This a is fun pocket version of cricket where you create your fantasy team and score runs by throwing dice. My opening batsman Smiffy (from the Bash Street Kids) plays a blinder until he's unluckily bowled out by Charles Hawtrey. I wonder whether I should have sent in Plug to open and perhaps saved Smiffy for the problem number-three spot, but that's cricket.

Resigned to our fate, we book ourselves in for dinner and actually have a pretty good meal consisting of a hearty beef casserole and mashed potato, washed down with a litre of red wine that clears away the slight sense of listlessness that had settled over us during the course of the afternoon.

The gîte is quite crowded, mostly with Belgians, and it seems that many walkers use Mérens as a base for excursions of a few days here and there. One thing about our situation is that however unkempt, hairy and smelly we may be we maintain the GR10 high-ground (so to speak) simply by virtue of being amongst the small and noble group of people who are 'going the whole way' or 'toute la route' as the French might say. We earn immediate respect amongst our trekking peers when they hear of our endeavour and we share a mutual bond of respect with other walkers who are also on the coast-to-coast highway. It's like being members of a small and very exclusive club.

The evening is brought to a rather brutal, if somewhat comical end, when Little Hitler stands on a table and announces to the whole room that someone has blocked one of the toilets most unpleasantly (or words to that effect) and that she has had to spend a long and uncomfortable time trying to unblock said toilet. A barely suppressed hint of a smile passes around the room, along with a few amused but surreptitious glances and as if sensing this she shouts even louder from her table top, demanding to know who the guilty party is; as if someone is actually going to put up their hand and say, 'Yes miss, it was me'. Her confrontational style wins her few friends and she is a stark contrast to the other more laid-back refuge guardians that we have met along the way. We think she is probably new to the job, or possibly on work experience, but whatever – she's got anger issues.

At 9.30 p.m. it's lights-out time and unsurprisingly this is one of those super-austere refuges that have no individual light switches in any of the rooms or dormitories. On the insomnia front you may as well throw me to the lions and I lie there, staring into the blackness, waiting for sleep to come.

Unfortunately, what does come isn't sleep but one of the worst cases of indigestion I have ever experienced, and I stagger through the darkness to find a toilet to see if that might provide me some relief. The ground-floor toilets are now all out of action, probably through some wanton act of revenge by our Nazi hostess, so I head downstairs to the very depths of the building with only a pathetically weak torch for company. I get totally lost in the darkness and at one point bump into someone coming the other way wearing a head-torch, like some kind of subterranean caver. We exchange muted greetings, grunts in the night, and he points me towards the toilet and then shuffles off as I watch his halo of light disappearing into the gloom. I could go mad down here. It's like a scene from *Alien*.

DAY 44

REFUGE DES BÉSINES TO LAKE OF MANY VOWELS

Three hours of sleep and I feel like my nerves have been stir-fried and served up on a bed of cold spaghetti. The place is busy with people breakfasting and faffing about with their rucksacks and boots and I just want to head out of here and get back on the move as quickly as possible. It's still raining and the temperature has also dropped considerably, but it is still with some relief that we leave the rather grim Refuge des Bésines behind with its power-crazed female commandant.

We have a long seven- or eight-hour stretch today, although amazingly a climb of only about 250 m, which doesn't seem right at all. We are on a kind of plateau area and the high point is the Col de Coma d'Anyell, which also marks the boundary between the Ariège and the Pyrenees Orientals, the Eastern Pyrenees. This is a poignant, symbolic moment, as we move out of the harsh wilderness of the Ariège and back into relative civilisation, and also marks the beginning of the final stage of our journey.

As we move into the Eastern Pyrenees and away from the high mountains we hope that we will leave some of the thunderstorms and rain behind us, the weather supposedly being calmer and steadier in the sweep down towards the coast. We are moving into Roussillon, and the high peaks of Andorra and those west of Mérens give way to the large, sweeping, shallower valleys of the Tét and Tech. Indeed, the only large peaks left to the east are the Pic du Carlit (2,921 m) and the Pic du Canigou (2,784 m).

The Roussillon region has a rich cultural history, arguably richer than other areas of the Pyrenees, possibly as a result of its greater accessibility and the virtual gateway it has provided across the mountains between France and Spain. Our aforementioned friend Hannibal passed through here back in 218 BC, fertilising the land as he went, and the Romans also used this region as a natural corridor to the Iberian Peninsula.

Then, of course, there were the Cathars, who established themselves in this south-west region of France around the twelfth century. This ill-fated sect of the Catholic Church followed a rather admirable purist and non-violent religious path, but the combination of their fundamentally different beliefs and rapid spread across the land led to some inevitably swift action by the Church, as the Pope sanctioned a brutal crusade against them. By 1244 the Cathar priesthood were more or less wiped out. Several hundred Cathars who refused to renounce their faith were burnt alive below the walls of the fortress at Montségur, just north of Ax-les-Thermes and not far from here.

We plan to camp tonight, despite the rather miserable weather, and it is a welcome change to have such an easy stage. Mind you, Rob's toes are causing him more and more pain and we stop every hour or so for an official toe break, which allows him to get his boot off and give them a bit of a stretch and massage. Rob now officially calls his big toe 'Ranulph' as in Fiennes, the mercurial adventurer who cut off a couple of his own toes with a hacksaw after they were damaged by frostbite. Fiennes also hacked off the fingertips on his left hand in his garden shed with a Black & Decker. Will it come to this I wonder? I sincerely hope not. Whatever the problem is with Rob's toes, it's a great shame as it really impacts upon Rob's experience of the walk.

We stop for lunch in a little shepherd hut, the Cabane du Solá, along with a few other people we have semi-hooked up with along the way. There is a youngish couple, from Belgium of course, whom we chat to a little and it sounds like they are rock climbers, out here for some serious mountaineering. The hut provides a little respite from the cold and we fire up our gas cooker to knock up some welcome hot soup.

The landscape flattens out as the valley opens up and we leave the mountains behind for the moment. The sun even puts in a rare appearance and we get out our wet shirts and hang them from the back of our rucksacks to dry as we walk. The walking is easy and soon we arrive at the Lac des Bouillouses, or the Lake of Many Vowels, as we call it. It's a pretty area and the lake and surrounding countryside is clearly a popular spot for day-trippers to drive up to and wander around. The lake itself it a result of the river being dammed and the large 'barrage' or dam is an impressive sight.

A huge building called 'Le Bones Hores' sits on the western side of the dam and seems to house a gîte, a restaurant and various other community offerings. It turns out that this place was built as a training centre for the French athletes in the run up to the 1968 Mexico Olympics, presumably for the water sport events like rowing and sailing. It's an ugly and rather incongruous place (well, that's 1960s architecture for you) and doesn't tempt us to stay, although we do have a rest and a beer or two in the bar. The plan is to walk on a little further, maybe an hour or so, and find a place to camp. Tomorrow, we plan to meet up with my brother and his family who, by coincidence, happen to be holidaying in the area and are happy to put us up for the night, all being well.

After another hour or so of walking we find a nice place by the side of the river and set up camp. We are now pretty efficient at this operation; I put up the tent and Rob knocks together his bivvy with the help of our walking sticks and several pieces of string. Then it's fire duty and we spend a fair bit of time trying to gather together enough wood. This is a well-used camping area and has been well scoured for anything burnable, but soon we have a small fire going. It's really quite cold tonight and we huddle around the fire, although the gusty wind ensures that we get well and truly smoked out.

During the night it gets even colder and even though I am in my sleeping bag and wearing all my clothes I am freezing. My cough has also got worse and so I lie in the cold hacking away and downing Nurofen. As is often case, I only finally feel comfortable and warm at about six in the morning and drift off for my precious two or three hours of sleep.

DAY 45

LAKE OF MANY VOWELS TO VILLEFRANCHE DE CONFLENT

With the usual post-camping fug – tired, cold, zipped-out and needing a lie down – we make some coffee and have some noodles and once we get moving I feel fine. The plan today is to walk to Mont-Louis, catch the 'Little Yellow Train' down to Villefranche de Conflent, and get picked up by my brother Jonathan, who has rented a house nearby. It's purely chance that our paths have crossed, but it will be good to meet up with him and his family, and a little bit of hospitality will be a welcome respite from weeks of bunkhouses and cold tents.

Many years ago, when Jess was around three years old, Nicky and I took a break from the rat race and lived for three months in a little place called Sorède, which was down at the coast near Argelès-sur-Mer and not really that far from here as the crow flies. During this trip we visited Mont-Louis, where we are headed now, and as we walk I start to recognise names and places on the map; it feels very strange to be entering into this familiar territory in such a profoundly different way and so many years later.

The walk itself today is an easy four or five hours with a gentle descent into Mont-Louis. We walk along easy woodland paths dotted with cows, horse riders and mountain bikers. There are lots of people about and we really have left the wilds of the Ariège far behind now, just about a week away from Banyuls. The end is in sight and that puts a little spring in our step as we saunter down towards the town.

Rob's toe is causing him more and more discomfort and the toe breaks have become more frequent, as he massages and kneads the pain out of his poor feet. Many people might have given up faced with this kind of daily pain, but not Rob. He's not a quitter and this walk has, for both of us, become about the achievement of getting to the end. At this stage, days away from our goal, nothing will stop us from getting there.

We amble into Mont-Louis, an attractive old fortified town with a commanding hilltop view across the Col de la Perche. The town is dominated by the amazingly pristine-looking fortress that was constructed under the watchful eye of Louis XIV's prolific military engineer Sébastien Le Prestre de Vauban. The Eastern Pyrenees are dotted with the solid and angular fortresses of Vauban, built in the 1600s to strengthen the border between France and Spain. In fact, Vauban was a hugely influential and industrious engineer, upgrading the fortifications of around 300 cities across France during the period between 1667 and 1707, as well as overseeing the building of thirty-seven new fortresses and military harbours. Having seen many of his forts during my travels around France, one is struck by his almost signature geometric angular design.

The Little Yellow Train or 'Le Petit Train Jaune' is for me one of the familiar experiences from times past, having taken a ride in it at least a couple of times all those years ago. The train is of the electric variety, powered by the hydroelectric generators on the River Tet; it's a cute, somewhat touristy narrow-gauge affair that runs from Mont-Louis to Villefranche de Conflent and includes a stop at Bolquère, the highest railway station in France. After bigging the train up a bit to Rob he is a little disappointed by the reality, hoping that it might have been a more genuinely authentic experience and, to be fair, he is right. The scenery is stunning but it does feel a little like travelling on some kind of theme park shuttle bus. Two of the carriages are open-topped, but we only manage to find space on a closed carriage and as it's busy we squat down by the door on our rucksacks. It feels a little like being on the Tube, apart from the small fact that we aren't travelling underneath London, and small children clutch their mother's hands and look at us cautiously as if we are some kind of strange yeti-like creatures, come down from the mountains for a little ride on the train with the humans. I guess that's not too far from the truth.

We disembark from 'Le Petit Train' at Villefranche de Conflent with a niggling awareness that we didn't buy a ticket back up at Mont-Louis and might be nabbed at any moment by the French train police, who in my experience are somewhat more zealous than their English counterparts. We saunter through trying to look inconspicuous, although with our massive rucksacks, wild beards and generally unkempt yeti-like appearance it's not that easy. But then maybe we benefit from a bit of reverse psychology in the sense that we stand out so much from the holidaying parents and children around us that the idea we might be fare-dodgers is just plain ridiculous.

Still, get through we do and as we file out amongst all the other passengers I catch sight of my brother Jonathan, who is following our progress through the lens of his camera, not realising that he is capturing a small crime in the making. Rob and I are well pleased; that's both the Luchon cable car and the Little Yellow Train that we have navigated *'sans argent'* so to speak. Many years ago I managed to 'jump' a cross-channel ferry from Dieppe to Newhaven, so all in all I am satisfied to be able to add a couple more unusual modes of transport to my fare-dodging escapades.

Villefranche de Conflent is another of Vauban's fortified towns, one of the more notable and important examples of his work. The town is tightly squeezed in within the original castle walls and dates back to 1098. Along with its UNESCO world listing it is classed as one of the most beautiful villages in France. Sitting high above the town is Fort Liberia, again fortified by Vauban, and with its superb vantage point across you can see that it must have protected this little town very well. The fort is connected to the town by a dramatic tunnel, built in the nineteenth century, which I remember exploring during my previous visit.

It's good to see Jonathan but also a little surreal that he is here, and I experience a psychological frisson of colliding worlds as I mentally navigate myself into a different social context. Jonathan, with his first sentence, manages to get in a reference both to the question of whether I had lost weight or not (the suggestion being that perhaps I needed to) and my resemblance to 'the old man', the only surprise being that he doesn't go for the hat-trick by remarking with mock surprise upon my lack of hair.

Ah, brothers, what would I do without them?

Anyway, Jonathan whisks us off to his holiday pad, which is a very nice house about twenty minutes away. His partner Sue and the kids are all in residence and I think both Rob and I feel swept over by this tide of family-ness. We eat well, have a few glasses of wine and Sue is a real star and does all our washing, which is no mean task. We eat out in the garden and the delightful children are clearly engaged by the sudden appearance of Uncle Dave and his friend Rob. Actually, many years ago and for some long-lost reason, Jonathan's children took to calling me 'Steve' and they are soon in full flow, deciding to add to the confusion by calling Rob 'Bob'. So, during the course of the evening we become the 'Steve and Bob Show' and this amuses them no end.

Rob is on good form and is particularly good with kids with his quick humour and natural playfulness. We drink more wine and the kids make more jokes about Steve and Bob until we are all bordering upon mild hysteria. Funnily enough, for many years the barman of our local pub used to call me Mike, and because I made the mistake of not correcting him straight away it got to the point where it was just too late and I had to let it go. And at the moment, there is a guy down at my allotment who calls me Pete, and once again it has somehow got beyond the point of putting him straight because he'll just ask, understandably, why I didn't say anything earlier.

So there you have it: Dave, Steve, Mike and Pete. I think I need to get seriously more assertive before I have a real crisis of identity. Still, Jonathan and Sue look after us very well and by the time we crash out we have been fed, watered, laundered and well prepared for the next stage of our journey. I still feel rough with this kind of fluey sore throat and I knock back a couple more Nurofen before finally hitting the sack.

DAY 46

VILLEFRANCHE DE CONFLENT TO REFUGE DU RAS DE LA CARANÇA

I actually sleep pretty well and after breakfast Jonathan kindly takes us back up to Mont-Louis so that we can continue where we left off yesterday. As he weaves his speedy way up the side of the valley we realise the amount of height we dropped down from on the train yesterday. Jonathan joins us for a quick coffee before heading off back down the valley, leaving the two of us to face the day ahead. According to Douggie we have a long ten- or eleven-hour stretch ahead and we decide to heed his advice and break the journey at the Refuge du Ras de la Carança, which is roughly around six hours from here. Rob looks a bit peaky and he tells me that he is suffering terribly from the journey and was only seconds away from throwing up in the back of Jonathan's car. Rob has always suffered a touch of carsickness and I guess not being in a car for such a long time and then being spun repeatedly around numerous hairpins has really done him in. Still, I am mighty glad that we managed to avoid an enclosed projectile-vomit situation.

We have another coffee to delay the inevitable but eventually the time comes when we heave on our rucksacks and head out of the town to find the dreaded trail. Once again it is hard to motivate ourselves as we tend to lose momentum with any break in our routine, both psychologically and physically. We walk for an hour or so along a small road through pleasant leafy woods, but even though we are following the trusty red and white GR10 trail markers Rob has a niggling feeling that not all is as it should be. He checks the maps, gets the lay of the land and realises that we are heading in the wrong direction. I tell him with absolute conviction we can't be; that the markers can't be wrong. Rob patiently shows me the map, the relief of the land and the orientation of our position and persuades me that he must be right, and of course he is.

It turns out we missed a turning a while back and have for the last hour been following the GR36, that goes god knows where. Lesson learned, I tuck my metaphorical tail meekly between my legs and we forlornly retrace our steps and finally pick up the GR10 again. It turns out the GR36 goes from the Pyrenees all the way across France to Ouistreham in Normandy. Now there's a journey for another day. Left to my own devices, I realise my map-reading blind spot would have led me completely up the garden path (or to Normandy anyway) and I am glad that Rob has his hand firmly on the GR tiller.

Whilst managing to orientate us in the right direction, Rob himself is still feeling physically disorientated from the car journey and he suffers waves of nausea. His feet are also continuing to cause him problems and to top it all he is getting bad stomach cramps and has a headache. It may be that he has picked up a bug or something, or perhaps his body has had enough of the daily battering it is getting as we climb up and down these bloody hills. He stops to commune with nature, so to speak, but it does little to alleviate his discomfort and to make matters worse we have a hell of an ascent up to Coll Mitja, the high point for the day. Coll Mitja itself is only about 800 m, but there are two smaller climbs we have to manage first and the overall amount of ascent adds up to around 1,200 m.

It's a killer and we make slow progress in the oppressive heat of the August sun, and whilst I feel OK physically, Rob is really hitting the proverbial wall today. The path climbs up through a pine forest, the air thick with its heavy scent, and the sun filters through picking out little glades that tempt us in with the promise of tranquil slumber. But like some kind of fairytale, I feel if we lie down to sleep in one of these places we may not wake again. So we press on and reach Pla de Cédeilles, the first high point of the day, and then head down the narrow, steep footpath that eventually crosses a small river and takes us past another small hut, the Refuge de l'Orry. We poke our heads in but it doesn't look too inviting and so we continue with our second bigger climb up to Coll Mitja.

It's steep, but eventually we reach the top and collapse for a while and top up our sugar levels with chocolate and oranges, our preferred fuel of choice at the moment. Then it's another hour of steep descent until we finally reach the Refuge du Ras de la Carança, which sits picturesquely in a clearing in the woods and alongside a river that tumbles down from the mountains. I seem to be thinking a lot about fairytales today and the scene reminds me of *Hansel and Gretel*, except without the witch and the breadcrumbs. It's also a good camping spot and a number of tents are dotted around the place, so I suggest that Rob takes the tent whilst I stay in the refuge. Rob isn't really up to a night in his homemade bivouac and I am happy to sleep in the dormitory, so the arrangement suits us both. The hut is basic and has no power but the friendly woman in residence knocks us up a hot chocolate and we sit outside and recuperate from the day's exertions. Rob then sticks the tent up and we eat soup and pasta al fresco as the day draws in around us.

As it gets dark Rob gets ready to hit the sack and I prepare to hit the dorm. There is an outside toilet a short walk around the back of the refuge. With no electricity and no plumbing the toilet is a very strange kind of green, chemical thing and as I sit on the pan I notice foot pedals, like those you might find on a pedalo boat, down on the floor by my feet. I try the pedals and hear a strange movement from down in the depths of the toilet. I glance down into the bowl in the gloom and realise there is a kind of conveyor belt contraption that moves along when you pedal. Ah, I get the idea now, although in a way I wish I hadn't. And so it is that I crap onto the conveyor belt and then pedal furiously until the noxious payload is eventually delivered over the edge into some unseen, chemical-filled container. This is certainly one of the stranger toilet experiences of my life (and I've had a few) and not one I fancy repeating. I feel my bowels beginning to contract in protest for another few days.

I wash my hands in the stream and back in the refuge I sit for a while in the corner writing my journal. The place is lit by candles and the only other people there are a small group of Italians and a couple of middle-aged French guys who are quietly working their way through a bottle of whisky. The voices wash around the small communal area, mellowed by candlelight and the gentle sound of the river outside. I really feel far away, in the middle of nowhere (which is exactly where I am) and it's strange to think that there is only one week left to go. I can't wait to get to Banyuls but I also want to enjoy this last week, somehow squeeze every last drop from the experience. Time is running away with itself, like the running water of the river outside. Will we get to Banyuls in one piece? I fantasise about a large gin and tonic and a swim in the sea. I can't wait to see Nicky and Jess.

DAY 47

REFUGE DU RAS DE LA CARANÇA TO PY

The plan today is to head for Mantet, which looks like it should take around four hours. After getting myself up I go out to find Rob and whilst he breaks camp I knock up some noodles for breakfast. We are both a little subdued. Rob still isn't feeling great and somehow he manages to both drop his breakfast and almost fall in the river as we set off.

The initial few kilometres are pretty good and take us up through the wooded valley until we hit the Col del Pal. From here we traverse the side of the valley and drop down towards Mantet and the last few hundred metres up to the village in the heat of the day is tough going. Mantet seems a nice enough place, although it sits on such a steep slope that just walking around the village is exhausting, so we find a little cafe and rest up for a quick drink. I feel a little queasy, down below, and make the most of the presence of a decent, pedal-free toilet. So far I have managed to avoid having to go in the woods, and although I accept that it is something of a rite of passage for a journey of this nature I am happy to delay it for as long as possible and will see it as a small victory if I can avoid it altogether.

After consulting the map, Rob hatches a plan that involves hitching down the hill to Py and from there walking the 750 m up to the Refuge de Mariailles that sits halfway up the next big ascent. It's still only early afternoon and seems like a good plan to me, especially as it would mean making up for some of the time we have lost.

We stand by the road that leads out of Mantet and amazingly the first car that comes along picks us up and takes us down to Py. They are a lovely young couple, very friendly and incredibly helpful, and they offer to take us all the way to the Refuge de Mariailles, although it is hard to know whether the road is good enough to get a car up there and we don't want them to go to too much trouble. It seems as if they would take us anywhere and that even if we said 'Banyuls!' they would probably consider it.

As we pull up in Py we consult the map and see how easy it might be for them to get us up to the refuge but in the end Rob decides he has had enough and is happy to call it a day and book into the gîte in Py; so we wave our friends off. A little bit of rest and relaxation is probably not a bad idea and I'm not going to argue the point, being quite happy to stay put here for the night. Py seems a nice, quiet little place, a characterful red-roofed village that nestles comfortably in the cradle of the valley, and we both look forward to a couple of beers and a bite to eat later.

The gîte is deserted, so we ring the manager and have a scrambled and nonsensical conversation on the phone. Some other people, a walking group of some sort, also start to arrive and it looks like they want to book in as well, so we all just sit around for an hour or so waiting for our man, as Lou Reed might say. Eventually, the man turns up and it seems the gîte is completely booked out by the group of walkers, who turn out to be Belgians, and although we try to argue the point it quickly becomes clear that there is no room at the inn. The owner suggests we try the village cafe/ restaurant that has rooms and so we saunter up there and ask the friendly woman who seems to be running the place. It seems like our luck has taken a bit of a hike itself today when the woman tells us that it's her grandfather's ninetieth birthday today and all the rooms in the cafe are taken up by the family who have arrived for the big night's celebration. She indicates a big building across the way that also has rooms and explains that they have all been taken up by the family. Jesus, this guy has a big family and it sounds like it is going to be one hell of a party. She suggests camping and indicates that there is a place down at the edge of the village we can camp; and so, rather reluctantly, we heave on our rucksacks and trundle down to the campsite that in fact turns out to be the play area of the village school. About right, I suppose, for a play therapist.

Py gets the thumbs up from both Rob and me and just nudges itself onto the list of 'Places We Could Live'. It's a sleepy, lived-in kind of place, small but large enough to have character in a somewhat lopsided kind of way. It has a scrappy kind of charm to it; even the church bells are discordant and out of tune, and this just endears us to the place even more. Rightly or wrongly, we pronounce Py as 'pie', and of course to live in a place called Pie would also be great. We say hello to a couple of little old ladies who are lovingly tending some gorgeous-looking allotments bursting with super-sized marrows and cucumbers, the soil a marvellously rich terracotta red. For a keen allottmenteer like myself this pushes Py several places up the esteemed 'des res' list.

Tucked away beneath the rather eccentric cafe is a tiny *épicerie*, only open for a couple of hours a day, and we buy a few things and order some fresh croissants for the morning. In the cafe itself we have a good meal washed down with red wine and beer, with only the minor distraction of the Belgians who clamber in and colonise a small section of the place. Irrationally and childishly, I take a dislike to them because of the fact they ousted us from the gîte (although to be fair we weren't exactly in situ when they arrived). They also smile and talk a lot, which in my book just about seals their fate (my book, as you know, is not a very cheery one). We do chat a little to the kindly woman running the cafe, a friendly, slightly dotty woman who works like a trooper with the help of one or two people who drift in and out of the kitchen. She explains that because she is working she has to miss her grandfather's big night. We express our shock and horror at this and try and persuade her to go, but it is clearly a case of needs must.

Later on I ring home and Jess tells me about her new contact lenses and about all the terrible jobs they have lined up for me when I get back, as a way of punishment for abandoning them. Nicky tells me about an outbreak of foot-and-mouth disease in Surrey, of all places, not too far from my workplace. Finally, full and a little drunk we head back to the children's playground for some much-needed sleep.

DAY 48

PY TO REFUGE DE MARIAILLES

I slept well last night and I'm starting to accept the fact that I sleep better in the tent than I do in the gîtes. Rob clearly has the right idea about camping and maybe I have to let go of all my wimpish anti-camping prejudices. We have breakfast back up in La Fontaine, the cafe where we ate last night, but our pre-ordered croissants appear to have gone missing, probably commandeered along with everything else in the village for granddad's party. Still, our friendly lady says she can knock up a couple for us and so we sit and drink coffee and hot chocolate and toy with our dry toast and jam until she returns with the aforementioned articles.

She seems pretty stressed-out and tells us that she had to cook dinner for the Belgian group last night, make up all the rooms for her grandfather's visiting family and to cap it all open up the little *épicerie* at 6.30 a.m. She tells us she only had two hours' sleep and she certainly looks well frazzled. All this plus the fact that she didn't even get to go to the party. We don't know what the story is here but this poor woman seems to be getting a bit of a rough deal on the old family front. She heads back into the kitchen and so hungrily, and with expectations high, we bite into the croissants and experience what can only be described as a small-scale pastry explosion as the croissants shatter into a thousand pieces and rain down upon the table (and over us) in a shower of flaky crumbs. These are, officially, the crumbliest, driest and undoubtedly worst croissants in the history of the known universe (OK, not verified in the *Guinness Book of Records* but I'd stake Dodger, my pet rabbit, on it). Our disappointment is tangible and our lady friend has rather fortuitously disappeared, perhaps slightly ashamed of her role in this small but scandalous moment in Py's long history. Still, we can't hold it against her and indeed can only admire the pragmatic way in which she tackles life's hardships. Undoubtedly, times are hard in these tiny, isolated villages and whilst we can breeze in and out and enjoy the restful tranquillity of these places a lot of the people who live here really do struggle on the poverty line.

We pack up our gear and leave Py behind us, content in the knowledge that we only have a short walk, maybe three hours, to our next stop, the Refuge de Mariailles. Rob is still feeling a little queasy from yesterday, which we put down to not having fully recovered from the hairy drive up to Mont-Louis with my brother, but he feels OK to press on. On the edge of Py, I see the house of my dreams; a perfect place in a perfect position. It is a lovely rambling double-fronted farmhouse, mid-nineteenth-century perhaps, oozing character and charm with its red-tiled roof and blue window shutters. A stream runs under the lane and through the garden, which is large and pleasantly unkempt. I can see what looks like a well at the end of the garden and a large vegetable patch which, like the allotments in the village, is bursting with a fine-looking selection of vegetables. The house is just far enough outside the village for it to feel away from everything but close enough for a morning stroll to the cafe. I am half tempted to knock on the door and make the owner an offer there and there, even though I have no money. We stand for a few minutes, looking longingly at the house, and then continue on our way. As anticipated, it's a pretty pleasant and undemanding three-hour walk, taking us up through woodland to the Col de Jou, which seems to be something of a congregation point for bikers, drivers, walkers and cyclists, and there is a veritable bustle of activity as people go about their various leisure pursuits. We cross paths with our Belgian friends and inevitably they are heading for the same refuge that we are; I wouldn't be surprised if they have taken the last few beds with their big group booking.

We stop for a spot of lunch, baguette and pâté, and then continue up a fairly easy track and it is only for the last hour or so that it turns into a stiffer climb as we approach the refuge. Minutes before we get there it starts to rain and this quickly turns into a full-on thunderstorm, so it is with some relief that we reach the refuge and take cover from the deluge. Once in, we sit and have a couple of beers whilst we consider our sleeping options. I decide to go ahead and book a bed for the night, but Rob would prefer to camp outside and goes to check out a good spot. However, it's still pissing down and wisely he decides to book a bed in the dorm. We kill time for the rest of the day by drinking beer and coffee, playing cards and dodging Belgians.

DAY 49:

REFUGE DE MARIAILLES TO CHALET DES CORTALETS

Hot chocolate and Frosties for breakfast – superb! We are sitting in the midst of an extremely large (numbers, not size) French family who seem to be busily planning an adventurous trip up Mt Canigou. It's a nice morning, the sun is shining and we set off in good spirits.

The first stage of the walk is pretty gentle as we traverse the edge of the valley through woodland and we make good progress. The Belgians are still with us and our paths cross here and there, so that we seem always to be just behind or just in front of them. We stop for a map consultation and Rob makes the radical suggestion of abandoning Douggie for the day (who advises a circuitous route around Mt Canigou) and instead going directly up and over the mountain. It's a great idea and we embrace it with gusto.

Despite all his bravado, that Douggie must really have been a bit of a wimp if he didn't have the spirit to take on Canigou. Mt Canigou is the highest mountain in the Eastern Pyrenees, standing at around 2,800 m, and as most of the GR10 takes us over the saddles or cols between peaks, the idea of actually climbing a proper mountain is very appealing. The walk up is surprisingly easy, a gentle ascent that really only picks up in height and difficulty over the last couple of hours. However, the last part of the climb is a real scramble, as we have to hoist and heave ourselves over the lip of the summit. The peak itself is a small plateau, maybe 10 m or so across, and as we pull ourselves up and over the edge we are greeted by the sight of about twenty people, all just sitting around, eating their lunch and taking in the view. It feels a little unreal and there is quietness in the air – perhaps offered in respect to the great mountain.

We also realise that there is another, easier trail leading up to the peak from the opposite face. But this is a real highlight; to be sitting up here close to 3,000 m drinking the rarefied atmosphere and taking in the 360-degree panorama. It is pretty cloudy and we can't really see that much, but it's the thought that counts.

A metal cross rises up dramatically from the summit, festooned with the yellow and orange stripes of the Catalan flag. Canigou has a special symbolic significance for the fiercely proud Catalans and apparently every year, during a ceremony called Flama del Canigou, a fire is lit at the summit and an all-night vigil is kept as torches lit from Canigou's fire are relayed across Catalonia. Like the Basques at the beginning of our journey, the Catalans have a strong, independent culture and a strongly expressed sense of independence and it feels right that our journey should begin and end with such a striking sense of cultural vibrancy. To celebrate our epic conquest of Canigou we break out the stove and knock up a hot chocolate, and the event is doubly celebrated by the fact that we beat our sometime Belgian companions up here in the process. Petty perhaps, but to me it's a small victory.

After a while we decide to head off and follow a pretty well-worn trail leading down from the summit. Through the clouds we catch glimpses of the great plain of Rousillon, which stretches away towards Perpignan and of the two river valleys, the Tet and the Tech, which carve their way through the landscape and open out as they reach the Mediterranean. Because of the thick cloud that sits heavily upon the broad shoulders of Canigou, we are still denied our first glimpse of the Mediterranean. But all the same, I am suddenly struck by strong memories of the few months that I spent in this region all those years ago with Nicky and Jess, and the sense that we have almost reached our destination is tangible.

We both feel invigorated by a sense of achievement and through all the ups and downs of the journey, I feel honoured to have shared this experience with Rob. He's a true friend and I am not sure that either of us would have, or could have, managed such a journey on our own. It has been an epic voyage and one that has forged a very special bond between us that will remain throughout our friendship.

There are quite a few people around on this section of the trail, the walk up to Canigou being pretty popular, and on the way down we share a few words with a friendly young French couple. After a few hours we reach the Chalet Refuge des Cortalets, a large place with a restaurant, bar and enough beds for at least a hundred people. There is a buzz about the place and it seems that many people travel up here from the surrounding regions and use it as a base for walking, climbing and of course skiing in the winter. Rob considers camping but decides in the end to sleep indoors and so we check ourselves in and book a meal for tonight. Before we do anything else we get a couple of beers and join the French couple outside. They are called Nikola and Blondine and it turns out they are both doctors from Normandy involved in research into Alzheimer's disease. We like them immediately and arrange to meet up together for dinner.

The process of finding our room, having a shower and generally sorting ourselves out seems to take an age, due to complex systems of shower tokens, meal vouchers and all sorts of other Refuge paraphernalia. It seems that we are sharing our dorm with a number of French people and a dog that has a whole bunk to itself. The bunkhouse has become a doghouse; but then nothing surprises me anymore. Anyway, after hanging around for bloody ages for the shower to be free, we eventually spruce ourselves up and head down for a pre-dinner beer or two.

We play cards for a while and I introduce Rob to an old family card game called 'Skat' that has a tendency to become a little frenetic and is a game in which I am known for my ferocity. Within the game, players can be penalised for making a mistake, taking too long and generally for anything that might be deemed worthy of punishment. As always with this game, we become embroiled in a heated debate about the rules. It's fun, but I think Rob is getting annoyed by my pedantic approach and faulty logic and so we wander out into the restaurant area. We have all been allocated seats at particular tables by the control freaks that run this place, and so to engineer being able to sit with Nikola and Blondine we do a sneaky bit of name swapping before everyone else turns up. Who knows what little social chain of events we may have put in motion here with our little bit of skulduggery.

Nikola has a sharp sense of humour, as does Rob, and the evening is quite a laugh. Nikola is as tall and thin as the proverbial rake and eats like the proverbial horse. I am sure if given the chance he would just carry on scoffing all night. Blondine, in contrast to Nikola, is short and dark-haired and somewhat demure in character, a counterpoint to her partner's gregarious and outgoing nature. Interestingly, it turns out that the two of them are doing the HRP trail and, even though they have no climbing experience and this is the first time they have undertaken a trek of this kind, it hasn't been a problem for them. They said they did lose a few days due to bad weather, but on these occasions just dropped down from the heights and joined the GR10 for small sections before linking back up with the HRP when the weather improved. So much for all the bloody books that stated you needed to be an experienced climber to do the HRP; that you needed crampons and ropes and all that stuff.

Rob and I feel a little cheated and that maybe, knowing what we do now, we might have traversed more sections of the HRP ourselves. Certainly, Rob would have enjoyed it, what with the ridge-walking and staying up on the higher ground, but I am not so sure whether it would have been quite my cup of tea. To be fair, I probably would have driven him mad through moaning about the lack of a decent place to kip.

DAY 50

REFUGE DE CORTALETS
TO AMÉLIE-LES-BAINS

Our sleep was disturbed by the French group who all got up at 3.30 a.m. Not only that; each one of them had set their mobiles onto different modes of alarm and so I woke up thinking I had been transported to a Buzz Lightyear convention. Surely they could have simply agreed for one of them to set their alarm and just quietly wake the others? Still, the dog slept well. As it happens, it turns out that they were heading off on a night climb up to Canigou to watch the sunrise from the summit. Fair play to them and I forgive them immediately for the rude awakening.

After breakfast and a chat with Nikola and Blondine we decide to walk together, initially following the GR10 but then taking the HRP to Amélie-les-Bains. It's a change of plan but makes sense because it means we will not have such a long day tomorrow. Also, it will be nice to walk with Nikola and Blondine for a while and try a section of the HRP.

The weather is gorgeous, a rich sun and gentle breeze, and the first couple of hours' walking are pleasant indeed as we traverse the side of the valley and make the gentle climb up to the Col de la Cirère, which sits at 1,731 m. We have lunch together, flaked out in the lush grass, and then leave the GR10 and head off on the HRP. This is a totally new navigational experience, in which Nikola takes a cursory look at the map, fixes upon a point in the far distance and sets off, as the crow flies. I feel a little bereft as we leave the red and white GR10 markers behind, but also acknowledge that I had become rather too attached to them over the last few weeks. I guess in a way they had become a constant for me, a reference point that brought a degree of comfort and security, but at the same time closed down any learning I might have made on the navigational front. We make good progress and Nikola and Blondine are good company. Nikola is good-humoured and has an infectious smile and Blondine is quiet but gently assured.

Somewhat ironically, this being our first experience of the HRP, we end with a killer six-hour road walk and as the heat gradually builds we all feel a little worse for wear. The last couple of hours nearly finish us off and our poor feet suffer from the relentless pounding upon the road surface, which radiates heat up at us like an oven. Rob's feet are causing him more and more pain and we stop for a toe break every half hour or so, but he soldiers on gallantly, trooper that he is. We leave Nikola and Blondine in a little village a few kilometres outside Amélie-les-Bains where they have planned to stay for the night and we continue down the hill to the town. We must have walked close to 28 km today and both feel on the verge of collapse, so it is with little guilt that we stick out our thumb and get a lift with a nice lady who takes us the last couple of kilometres down the hill and into civilisation.

DAY 50

Amélie-les-Bains is a reasonably large, bustling kind of place and after a bit of ringing around we discover that the one campsite is full. We are hitting the French holiday season now and have noticed many more people around and about over the last few days, particularly as we approach the Mediterranean coast. Reverting to Plan B, we find a room in a cheap hotel and then do a bit of shopping and wash our clothes in a launderette. This will probably be the last clothes washing session of the trip and everything we do now is assuming certain significance as we approach the end of our journey.

Chores completed we head out to get a bite to eat and find a nice cafe where we can sit outside and take in the atmosphere. We are both so knackered from the day's walking that we feel almost stupefied, and as I sit watching the evening scene unfold in front of me I feel kind of detached from the whole experience, as if I am only partly in this world. I eat steak and chips and Rob has a rather good-looking couscous and chicken dish and we wash it down with a few beers. God, the recuperative powers of food and beer are astounding and we soon find ourselves returning to relative normality.

The town is a little like Eastbourne, full of elderly and for some reason very strange-looking people. This may sound harsh, both on Eastbourne and the elderly, but we are struck by the amazing specimens of humankind parading before us. Garish make-up, stretched faces, fake tans and Botox by the bucket load seem to be the order of the day. Of course, we soon realise that this is a spa town and the older generation have descended here in their masses to take in the rejuvenating water and regenerate their aged bodies. Further research tells us that indeed Amélie-les-Bains is a renowned 'health resort' and very popular with the oldsters.

After our meal we move off and find a another place for a drink, a kind of old dance hall that has an accordion player who is pretending very badly to play to a cheesy backing track and a barman who looks just like Uncle Fester from the Addams Family. We then spend at least an hour discussing the relative merits of *The Addams Family* versus *The Munsters* and working our way through the various characters. This place wraps itself around us with a warm surreal fug of nonsense and we both drift off into some 1920s French period comedy.

DAY 51

AMÉLIE-LES-BAINS
TO LAS ILLAS

It's my birthday today and also a national holiday in honour of the Assumption of the Blessed Virgin Mary. So Mary and I are sharing a special day. It's one of the odder birthday mornings I have experienced, as I wake up, having slept badly in the stifling heat, and survey the cheap hotel room with its peeling wallpaper and bleached light. It's OK though; it's got character.

We get suited and booted and head out to get some breakfast, which consists of coffee and some decent croissants that we buy in the patisserie and smuggle into the cafe. We spot Nikola and Blondine and call them over and they wish me a hearty happy birthday, which is nice. Nikola's humour is as sharp as ever and Blondine is quiet in her calm, self-confident way. Our plan today is to do another section of the HRP and we splash out on a 1:25 map. I feel insecure away from my trusty red and white GR10 markers and I am in full agreement with Rob that a decent map for this section would be a good idea.

We head off with Nikola and Blondine and as we climb up and away from the town the views are as stunning as ever. Behind us the town lies nestled amongst the rippling, green tree-covered hills and the contrasting effect of light and shade creates a lovely quality of depth to the scene, giving a tangible sense of the relief of the landscape.

As we reach the height of the day's walk we cross over into Spain for a short while and stop for a drink in an amazing old building that we think was once a monastery. Perhaps it's psychological, but having crossed the border everything feels very different; there's a tangible sense of being in another country and just the experience of sitting in this place, having to ask for our drinks in Spanish is strangely wonderful. Rob and I have a feeling that we could really get to like the Spanish side of things. It would have been nice to have spent more time here during the walk, perhaps to have linked up more with the GR11 that traverses the Spanish side of the Pyrenees.

For better or worse, I think perhaps I became somewhat wedded to the GR10 and the idea that this was the route we should follow, come what may. Rob perhaps was more open to the idea of moving between the GR10, the HRP and the GR11; and I think probably he was right. I guess for me it has been about holding onto something I know and sticking with it from start to end, but in doing so there is always the risk of losing sight of other possibilities. In a sense, this symbolises something about my life and my wariness about taking risks and exploring new challenges. I stick pretty much to the path, all in all, with the odd excursion here and there into new territory; by playing it safe one has to confront the possibility of regret and as I reflect upon my journey, my 'Grande Randonnée' through life, this is something that I feel poignantly. Blimey, maybe it's my birthday that's the cause of all this introspection; another year older and all that. Anyway, we sit in the beautiful garden of this quirky Spanish monastery with Nikola and Blondine and have a little birthday toast and it's a great place to be.

Reluctantly, we set off again and weave our way downward and back into France, passing the landmark that is the Roc de Frausa (the Roc de France) from which apparently one can get a first glimpse of the Mediterranean. We can't, though, for all our looking. The descent continues until we reach the village of Las Illas, a small, quiet place that has a rather gentle feel about it. There is a hotel in the village with a bar and restaurant and we stop for a drink as we take stock of our progress.

We meet a young friendly English guy who has also been walking coast to coast. His walking companion injured his foot a couple of weeks ago and so he decided to carry on by himself. We finish our drinks and then as we book into the *gîte d'étape* that is run by the friendly Madame Martinez, a slightly eccentric woman who lives just down the road, we meet three English women in their fifties who again have walked all the way from Hendaye. They are a very chipper group of middle-class women from East Sussex and it turns out that one of them is a physiotherapist working in Crowborough, my home town and where my mother still lives – small world. Suddenly three middle-aged men burst in and it turns out they are the husbands of this little group, having flown out to walk the last couple of days with their wives. Suddenly the gîte is bustling with middle-class, middle-England activity. It's all very touching really and there is a buzz in the air as we reach the climax of this venture, mixed with a palpable sense of relief that soon it will all be over.

Rob says that as it's my birthday I can decide what we do tonight. Truth be told, the options are limited and it comes down to a toss-up between a meal in the hotel restaurant or a beer and hot-dog shindig that's going on down at the other end of the village, in honour of the Blessed Virgin. Going for a meal seems to be the right thing to do on one's birthday so we walk into the restaurant where we get shown to a table and proffered a couple of menus.

The place is pretty empty; Nikola and Blondine are in one corner with Blondine's parents and our English chap is sitting on his own at another table. A few other people are scattered around but it all seems very civilised and just a little formal. We exchange a knowing look and then, before the critical point arrives, i.e. the waiter coming to take our order, we up sticks and get the hell out of there. This is no place to celebrate my birthday when all the locals are having a good old traditional knees-up down the road.

We stroll down through the village and past the *boulodrome*, where a hard-fought match is underway, and into a large open area where a dodgy-looking DJ and his teenage assistant are setting up their PA. I ask Rob if he thinks the DJ is a paedophile and he gently alludes to my somewhat twisted outlook on life. It's true, of course. The stage is a massive affair of scaffolding and lights and enough speakers to do Notting Hill Carnival proud. When it comes to the sound-check they blast out an impressive volume and we can't quite believe that enough people are going to turn out to justify their efforts. But these local fêtes always defy one's expectations.

Over the course of the evening a steady stream of children, teenagers, families and old folks casually saunter along and soon enough the place is buzzing with dancing, drinking and very cheesy Euro-music. At the bar, set up along one side of the field, we buy a bottle of wine and sit on a bench and watch the scene unfold. We are part of this, but also outsiders, yet our presence is welcomed without question. We get ourselves hot dogs (a good local sausage in a chunk of French bread) and they slip down very well with the red wine. As it's my birthday we splash out and get ourselves another bottle of wine and another hot dog.

By midnight the place is rocking, The DJ and his young assistant are lording it around and the two teams from the game of boule we watched earlier are getting totally smashed at the bar. In fact, the whole population of the village is well and truly tanked, but in a happy, civilised and very French kind of way. Ah, yes, this is the place to be.

DAY 52

LAS ILLAS TO PIC DES QUATRE TERMES

Bleary-eyed from the evening's efforts we knock ourselves up some coffee and prepare for what is the penultimate day of our trek. Everyone is slightly demob happy, a little mania creeping in with the anticipation that tomorrow afternoon we will be able plunge into the Med with reckless abandon. The Sussex ladies and their doting hubbies fuss around with an excessive degree of zeal and head off half an hour or so before us. The other English guy also sets off and soon after that we do too. Rob's toes are causing him more and more pain and the periodic toe breaks are now a routine part of our day. We haven't seen Nikola and Blondine and assume they must have set off earlier, or perhaps are resting up in the hotel where they stayed last night.

The first couple of hours are fairly easy, following a small tarmac lane that spiders its way gently uphill. It's hot and we feel knackered but at one point, as we round a bend near Col de Priourat, we catch our first glimpse of the sea. Bloody amazing!

The last time we saw the sea was just over seven weeks ago as it disappeared behind the Basque mountains.

From here we walk for another hour or so until we reach Perthus, a crummy shit-hole of a town that is only good for a brief drink-stop before continuing on our way. Perhaps I am being unfair, but I remember Perthus from my previous stay in this area and it hasn't changed. It's a border town and in fact the border between France and Spain runs down the main street. Tax in Spain is much lower than in France and so the place is full of people stocking up on booze, fags, petrol and whatever else they can cram into their cars. So it's pretty much your functional kind of border-town with little charm and it makes me feel like I am trapped in some kind of giant pound-shop, though I am sure that Perthus does have its good side, somewhere. It's also very busy, with a bloody great motorway running through it, and somehow the noise of the cars and lorries shatters the peace of the last few weeks and in a sense symbolises something about the end of this journey and our return to modern life.

From Perthus, the GR10 takes us on a 750-m climb up a tedious road and, to make matters worse, it suddenly starts pissing down. Rob makes a shelter by attaching our ponchos to some trees and we decide to sit and have a bite to eat and wait out the rain. After half an hour or so we set off again and, eventually, after about three more hours, we reach the *gîte d'étape*, the Chalet de Albere, which sits just below the Col de l'Ouillat. This being our last night on the road Rob suggests that we camp, to get a last taste of the mountain life, and it's a good idea. He has seen a little place on the map about another hour from here that looks like it might be a good place to stop. Our current walking companions, Nikola and Blondine and the Sussex ladies are all staying here, however, and as there is a nice bar in the gîte we stop for a beer and a chat. It would be easy to stay, too easy, and so with a little effort we drag ourselves away and head off towards the Pic des Quatre Termes, our chosen spot for the night.

From the gîte we climb up through some woods and then skirt around the perimeter of some kind of huge radio transmitter that sits on the Pic Neulos which stand at 1,256 m. From this point it's pretty much downhill all the way to Banyuls and it's almost impossible to believe that we haven't got any more horrendous climbing to do.

We are walking in a small range of low-lying mountains called the Albères, essentially the last foothills of the Pyrenees, and again I remember this area well from the time I spent here with Nicky and Jess all those years ago, when we endearingly called these hills the 'Old Bears'. In fact, as I look down over the plain of Rousillon I can more or less pick out where Sorède, the little village where we lived for three months, would lie. It's so strange to be here again, but in such a different way. As I look down I can see into the past; see Nicky and me drinking coffee with hot milk in the pretty village square whilst Jess runs around the fountain chasing baby crocodiles (lizards to you and me – baby crocodiles to a small child). Their presence now is tangible, they're literally just a few hours away and I give them a little wave.

The Pic des Quatre Termes was a good choice by Rob. We find a little picnic area sheltered by some trees and a firepit with a table next to it. With all my moaning over the weeks about having to camp and the seductive desires of a nice warm hotel room, it feels right that the two of us should spend our last night under the stars, enveloped by the darkening mountains.

We get the tent and bivvy up and then make a fire, although this isn't easy as the wood is damp due to the recent rain and hard to get going. We haven't got any paper with us and the only way we are going to get the fire going is to burn one of the maps. Again this seems a little symbolic as the maps (and the map-reading therein) have been the one thing that has caused a little tension between Rob and me. We choose a section of the walk that was the least exciting and use the map to get the fire going. There must be some kind of laminated quality to the paper because it burns vigorously and does the job. The fire burns, we cook up some soup and noodles and drink a couple of beers that we bought earlier in the bar back at the gîte. We even have a singsong with the ukulele, finished off with a comforting hot chocolate, and it's with an odd mixture of excitement, relief and just a little sadness that I climb into my sleeping bag for the last time.

'Night, Rob.'

'Night, Dave.'

Like the Waltons, our voices reach out into the night. We have had our differences over the last seven and a half weeks, ups and downs both literally and emotionally, but I know I couldn't have made this trip without Rob and it's a measure of our friendship that we have got through it without killing each other. We have both irritated the hell out of each other at times, but then one could expect little else having lived in each other's pockets for so long. But we have had a laugh, had adventures, met some great characters along the way and both been part of a journey that will stay with us forever, one way or another.

DAY 53

PIC DES QUATRE TERMES
TO BANYULS SUR MER

The hypothesis that I sleep better when we camp holds strong. So, this is it. The last day on the road. The last day of Vaselining my feet: of rummaging through my rucksack to find the least crusty socks and the least dirty shirt. The last day of heaving my rucksack onto my aching body and the sensation of the straps digging into various parts of my anatomy. We finish off the hot chocolate and suddenly I feel my bowels calling to me – it's that time of the morning. Bollocks! I've walked 850 km without once having to resort to having a crap in the woods but now, on the last day of all days, the time has come and can't be avoided, delayed or postponed in any kind of way.

'Don't forget to set fire to the paper,' Rob calls out after me, enjoying the moment. Deed done, I am walking out of the woods and suddenly all hell breaks loose; I am lost in thought, gently contemplating life's rich tapestry when I hear Rob suddenly shouting, 'Dave! Dave! *Sanglier!*' I quickly look up and can't see Rob; no, there he is near the bushes. It's bit late to be practising his French again. 'Dave!' he yells again, *'Sanglier!'* And then suddenly I see it: the back end of a wild boar charging out of the camp, its hairy arse quickly disappearing into the shrubbery. Bloody hell! We are both stunned, speechless for a moment and then break out with hoots of excited laughter. Rob tells me he was relieving himself in the bushes when he suddenly heard a noise and found himself face to face with the beast, which then turned on its hooves and shot off like a hairy, boar-shaped bullet.

We couldn't have wished for a more perfect start to our final day. The spirit of the *sanglier* has been with us right from day one, when Rob first started popping them into his little kettle, and there is a marvellous sense of serendipity about our lively encounter this morning. I learn later that the wild boar is a symbol of intrepidness, bravery and perseverance and indeed what better symbol could there be to capture the essence of our adventure across these mountains.

It's about six hours to Banyuls, downhill all the way, more or less, and we set off in a good mood, our spirits buoyed by our rather surreal close encounter with the *sanglier*. I feel increasingly lost in my own thoughts as we continue, imagining the moment of seeing Nicky and Jess for the first time in a month and a half. A lot of the walking today is through open scrubland and parts of the route aren't that well marked. We had an hour or so head start on the others, who stayed back in the gîte last night, and we left reasonably early so we don't see them for a while; but later, as we rest and have a bit to eat, the Sussex Ladies come by with their hubbies in tow. No sign of Nikola and Blondine; they are obviously taking it easy today.

The route takes us up to Pic Sailfort (a lowly 981 m) and from here we get our first view of Banyuls. It looks bloody miles away, a tiny Lego town in the distance and there is still a range of foothills to negotiate before we get anywhere near it. But all the same, it's a great sight. We stop for a bite to eat and I call Jess on my mobile and give her our estimated time of arrival. She sounds so close and they have made base camp in a cafe by the beach with Nicky's brother David who has come over with them.

From the Pic Sailfort we have to pick our way down through a winding rock path that descends steeply in places. It's hard going and requires concentration, but eventually we drop down to the Col de Baillaury. Rob's feet are killing him and the toe breaks are becoming ever more frequent as he desperately tries to massage away the pain. Thank god this is the last day, because I'm really not sure if his feet could take much more of this. We keep dropping down and reach another spot called the Col de Llagastera where there is a sign that says 'Banyuls 1 hr 20 min'. The end really is in sight now as the town steadily grows in size and the last of the Pyrenean foothills sweep down majestically towards the blue sea.

The last few kilometres take us on a gentle path that zigzags down through a series of leafy vineyards and we stop now and again to pick a few grapes from the vines that grow along the edge of the path. They taste sweet; and all the sweeter for the fifty-three days and 850 km we have travelled to pick them. The rusty red roofs of Banyuls get ever closer and the blue of the Mediterranean provides an increasingly alluring backdrop. As we approach the outskirts of town we see Blondine's parents waiting by the side of the road, a touching reception committee for their daughter and son-in-law. They take photos of us as we approach them and then we greet each other, as vigorously as if they are our own parents. We are all joined now by our mutual endeavour, partners in a shared experience. We tell them that Nikola and Blondine shouldn't be long now and then looking back we see them, little specks in the distance.

Suddenly we are walking into the outskirts of Banyuls and even at this point poor Rob's feet are hurting so much that he needs to take another toe break. The route takes us down by the railway and through a kind of tunnel under the line where we emerge into the heart of the town. The blood pounds in my head as we head towards the sea and I feel light-headed and dizzy in the knowledge that the walk is over and ecstatic at the expectation of seeing my family. Before I know it we reach the beach and we stride across the pebbles towards the water and as we do so I hear shouts from somewhere behind us. I turn my head and see Nicky and Jess running at us at speed and the next few minutes are a whirl of intense, joyful emotion such as I've never quite experienced before. Rob and I are enveloped in their warm embrace; I hug and kiss them with abandon and we all have tears in our eyes. They both look gorgeous. And then there is only one more thing to be done. I drop my rucksack to the ground for the last time and plunge headlong into the cool, refreshing Mediterranean water.

Coast to coast: from the Atlantic to the Mediterranean along 850 km of mountains. This, then, really is the end. I emerge from the water bearded and bedraggled, clothes dripping and faint with happiness, and it's more hugs all round. The Sussex ladies come over and we all congratulate each other, bonded by our unique endeavour. And now Nikola and Blondine appear for another round of celebratory hugs and handshakes. Whether or not we see these good people again, this has been a unique experience that bonds us to each other forever in our collective memories. And then Rob and I and Nicky and Jess just hold and look at each other, the four of us, trying to take it in. I meet Rob's eyes and we glance up at the cafe on the beachfront. Time for a quick beer?

EPILOGUE

The days following the end of our trek passed in something of a blur, as we slowly adapted to the idea of standing still. The morning after we arrived in Banyuls, Rob and I took ourselves off to a coiffeur and had our beards ceremoniously removed. The lady coiffeuse herself seemed bored and particularly unmoved by the experience and I wondered for a moment whether the hair salons of Banyuls are subjected to an endless stream of hairy, grubby men all relieving themselves of two months' worth of unkempt facial hair. That's a lot of beards to sweep up. I could have shaved myself I suppose, but this seemed the right way to approach the matter in hand. My beard had become something of a symbol of the journey – the passage of time, growth perhaps – and apparently made me look a little like my father, himself something of a hairy hiker in his day. Still, it was a pleasure to be able to sit back and be transformed back into my former self. Rob of course had already lost his beard once back in Luchon in an effort to capture the heart of the lovely Celine, but being the virile type had already caught me up.

As for our fellow GR10ers, we learned later that Craig and Lucy decided to call it a day somewhere around the Cauterets area, the result of sore feet and dwindling motivation. Corinne also threw in the towel and got as far as St Girons before heading back to Paris. Hans and his nameless daughter, Shepherd Boy, Camping Guy and assorted others had I guess all been discharged earlier onto Banyuls beach and gone their separate ways. I feel very honoured to have met such a sparkling array of characters along the way and they all contributed to making this journey a unique and memorable experience. If any of them pick up this book one day and stumble across themselves, as it were, I hope they can accept it in the good spirit that it was intended.

Do I hate walking? No, I don't think so. But I don't think I could have undertaken this venture on my own and owe a debt of eternal gratitude to Rob for his fine company. I couldn't have asked for a better companion. The charity cricket match went ahead a couple of weeks after our return and, much to Rob's chagrin, saw another victory for my merry band of cricketing journeymen, the Surbiton Swingers. But, to be fair, his team have more than made amends since and there is a forlorn space on my mantelpiece where the Ashes should be.

And as for Nicky and Jess – well, what can I say? They indulged my grand whim, my mid-life folly, and I was suitably punished on my return by the arrival of a black Labrador puppy (thankfully not a *pastou*). I had resisted this for years but somehow seem to have lost all my bargaining chips somewhere in the Ariège. Oh well. Anyway, I suppose I should mention something to them about the GR20, the long-distance coast-to-coast trail across Corsica...

Have you enjoyed this book?
If so, why not write a review on your favourite website?

If you're interested in finding out more about our travel books
friend us on Facebook at **Summersdale Traveleditor**
and follow us on Twitter: **@SummersdaleGO**

Thanks very much for buying this Summersdale book.

www.summersdale.com